Elementary Science Methods

An Assets-Based Approach to Teaching, Learning, and Advocacy, Grades K–6

■ ■ ■

Lauren Madden

The College of New Jersey

ROWMAN & LITTLEFIELD
Lanham • Boulder • New York • London

Executive Acquisitions Editor: Mark Kerr
Assistant Editor: Courtney Packard
Sales and Marketing Inquiries: textbooks@rowman.com

Credits and acknowledgments for material borrowed from other sources,
and reproduced with permission, appear on the appropriate pages within the text.

Published by Rowman & Littlefield
An imprint of The Rowman & Littlefield Publishing Group, Inc.
4501 Forbes Boulevard, Suite 200, Lanham, Maryland 20706
www.rowman.com

86-90 Paul Street, London EC2A 4NE

British Library Cataloguing in Publication Information Available

Library of Congress Cataloging-in-Publication Data
Names: Madden, Lauren, author.
Title: Elementary science methods : an assets-based approach to teaching, learning, and
    advocacy, grades K–6 / Lauren Madden.
Description: Lanham, Maryland : Rowman & Littlefield, [2022] | Includes bibliographical
    references and index.
Identifiers: LCCN 2021045547 (print) | LCCN 2021045548 (ebook) | ISBN
    9781538127117 (Cloth : acid-free paper) | ISBN 9781538127124 (Paperback : acid-
    free paper) | ISBN 9781538127131 (ePub)
Subjects: LCSH: Science—Study and teaching (Elementary)—Standards—United States.
    | Curriculum planning—United States. | Educational accountability—United States. |
    Next Generation Science Standards (Education)
Classification: LCC LB1585.3 .M33 2022 (print) | LCC LB1585.3 (ebook) | DDC
    372.35/0440973—dc23/eng/20211103
LC record available at https://lccn.loc.gov/2021045547
LC ebook record available at https://lccn.loc.gov/2021045548

Contents

■ ■ ■

Foreword   xi

Acknowledgments   xiii

1 An Introduction to Assets-Based Elementary
   Science Teaching   1
   CHAPTER 1 SUPPLEMENTARY LESSON:
     COOKIE CHEMISTRY LESSON   7

2 A Developmental Perspective on Science Teaching
   and Learning   15

3 Inquiry-Based Teaching: Connecting Theory to Strategy   27

4 What Is (and Isn't) Science Anyway?   39

5 The Next Generation Science Standards: An Introduction   51

6 Asking Good Questions and Developing Lessons   63
   CHAPTER 6 SUPPLEMENTARY LESSON:
     TERMITE TRAILS LESSON   73

7 Connecting Science to Language Arts and Mathematics   79
   CHAPTER 7 SUPPLEMENTARY LESSON A:
     HORSESHOE CRAB LESSON   90
   CHAPTER 7 SUPPLEMENTARY LESSON B:
     BATTLESHIP WIND FARM   93

8   STEM and STEAM: Creativity and Problem-Solving
in Elementary Science   97
    CHAPTER 8 SUPPLEMENTARY LESSON:
      RIDE OR DIATOM LESSON   114

9   Beginning to Use Science to Advocate   119

10 Equity, Diversity, and Inclusion in Science Teaching   133

11 How Do We Know What We Know in Science?   147

12 Science Outside of School   159

13 Advocating for Science   173

Glossary   179

References   183

Index   191

About the Author   201

Detailed Contents

■ ■ ■

Foreword   xi

Acknowledgments   xiii

1   **An Introduction to Assets-Based Elementary Science Teaching**   1

   ADVOCATING FOR SCIENCE   3

   SCIENCE INSIDE THE ELEMENTARY CLASSROOM   4

     An Activity for Teachers   4

     Reflecting on Your Exploration   6

   CHAPTER 1 SUPPLEMENTARY LESSON: COOKIE CHEMISTRY LESSON   7

2   **A Developmental Perspective on Science Teaching and Learning**   15

   JOHN DEWEY (1859–1952)   18

     Implications for Science Teaching   19

   JEAN PIAGET (1896–1980)   20

     Implications for Science Teaching   22

   LEV VYGOTSKY (1896–1934)   22

     Implications for Science Teaching   24

   PUTTING THE PIECES TOGETHER   24

     An Activity for Teachers   24

CONCLUSION 25

3 Inquiry-Based Teaching: Connecting Theory to Strategy 27
 AN EXAMPLE ACTIVITY 28
 INQUIRY-BASED SCIENCE INSTRUCTION 29
  The Continuum of Inquiry 30
  Foundations for Inquiry-Based Science 32
  But Why Inquiry? 32
 STRATEGIES FOR INQUIRY-BASED SCIENCE TEACHING 33
  Learning Cycle Models for Inquiry-Based
   Science Teaching 34
  Phases of Inquiry Model 35
  Discrepant Events 36
  Is Inquiry the Only Way? 36
 CONCLUSION 37

4 What Is (and Isn't) Science Anyway? 39
 SCIENTIFIC INVESTIGATIONS USE A VARIETY OF METHODS 42
 SCIENTIFIC KNOWLEDGE IS BASED ON EMPIRICAL EVIDENCE 43
 SCIENTIFIC KNOWLEDGE IS OPEN TO REVISION IN LIGHT
  OF NEW EVIDENCE 43
 SCIENTIFIC MODELS, LAWS, MECHANISMS, AND THEORIES
  EXPLAIN NATURAL PHENOMENA 43
 SCIENCE IS A WAY OF KNOWING 44
 SCIENTIFIC KNOWLEDGE ASSUMES AN ORDER AND
  CONSISTENCY IN NATURAL SYSTEMS 45
 SCIENCE IS A HUMAN ENDEAVOR 47
 SCIENCE ADDRESSES QUESTIONS ABOUT THE NATURAL
  AND MATERIAL WORLD 47
 TEACHING SCIENCE AT THE ELEMENTARY LEVEL 48
 AN EXAMPLE 48
 CONCLUSION 49

5 The Next Generation Science Standards: An Introduction 51
 STANDARDS ARE NOT CURRICULUM 52
 SCIENCE STANDARDS IN THE UNITED STATES 53
 THE NEXT GENERATION SCIENCE STANDARDS (NGSS) 54
  Disciplinary Core Ideas 56
  Crosscutting Concepts 57

Science and Engineering Practices   58

Reading the NGSS   60

Using the NGSS   61

A Challenge   62

CONCLUSION   62

6 Asking Good Questions and Developing Lessons   63

PRODUCTIVE QUESTIONS   64

Attention-Focusing Questions   64

Measuring and Counting Questions   64

Comparison Questions   64

Action Questions   64

Problem-Posing Questions   65

BLOOM'S TAXONOMY   65

OTHER MODELS FOR QUESTIONING   66

UNCOVERING STUDENT THINKING USING QUESTIONING   67

PLANNING INSTRUCTION   68

Backward Design   69

CONCLUSION   72

CHAPTER 6 SUPPLEMENTARY LESSON:
TERMITE TRAILS LESSON   73

7 Connecting Science to Language Arts and Mathematics   79

ENGLISH LANGUAGE ARTS   82

MATHEMATICS   86

USING THE STANDARDS TO HELP BUILD
INTEGRATED LESSONS   88

CHAPTER 7 SUPPLEMENTARY LESSON A:
HORSESHOE CRAB LESSON   90

CHAPTER 7 SUPPLEMENTARY LESSON B:
BATTLESHIP WIND FARM   93

8 STEM and STEAM: Creativity and Problem-Solving in Elementary Science   97

WHAT IS STEM ANYWAY?   98

The Engineering Design Process   98

Some Examples of STEM in Elementary Classrooms   100

STEM and Failure   104

STEM AND THE NGSS   105
   A Challenge to Teaching STEM in Science   107
STEAM   108
   Communication   110
   Community Building   111
   Content Explanation   111
   Creative Expression   112
CONCLUSION   113
CHAPTER 8 SUPPLEMENTARY LESSON:
   RIDE OR DIATOM LESSON   114

9 Beginning to Use Science to Advocate   119
SCIENTIFIC ARGUMENTATION   121
SOCIOSCIENTIFIC ISSUES   122
CONTROVERSIAL IDEAS IN SCIENCE   123
INTRODUCING SCIENCE AND SCIENTISTS TO THE
   ELEMENTARY CLASSROOM   126
A SENSE OF PLACE   129
CONCLUSION   132

10 Equity, Diversity, and Inclusion in Science Teaching   133
DIVERSITY IN SCIENCE AND ENGINEERING   134
FAMILY ENGAGEMENT   138
ANTI-RACIST SCIENCE TEACHING   139
SCIENTIFIC VOCABULARY   140
AN ASSETS-BASED APPROACH TO SCIENCE   141
SCIENCE TEACHING AS AN INCLUSIVE PRACTICE   142
   Universal Design for Learning   142
CONCLUSION   146

11 How Do We Know What We Know in Science?   147
TEACHER-CREATED ASSESSMENT   150
   Selected-Response Items   150
   Constructed-Response Items   151
   Portfolio or Performance Assessments   152
USING RUBRICS AND CHECKLISTS   153
FORMATIVE ASSESSMENT   154
   Formative Assessment before Instruction   154

Formative Assessment during Instruction   155
Formal Formative Assessment   155
Informal Formative Assessment   156
Exemplar Formative Assessment Strategies   156
A CHALLENGE   157
CONCLUSION   158

12 **Science Outside of School**   159
INFORMAL SCIENCE AND THE NGSS   161
Venues for Learning Science outside the Classroom   161
EVERYDAY LEARNING: JOEY   163
DESIGNED ENVIRONMENTS: THE FRANKLIN INSTITUTE   165
PROGRAMS: PARKWAY ELEMENTARY SCHOOL'S
ENVIRONMENTAL STEM CLUB   166
THE OPPORTUNITY GAP: WHY INFORMAL SCIENCE
LEARNING DESERVES ATTENTION   168
CONCLUSION   171

13 **Advocating for Science**   173
ADVOCATING FOR A CAUSE   175
Connecting across Content Areas   175
Current Events and Relevant Issues   176
STEPS FOR CLASSROOM PRACTICE   176

Glossary   179

References   183

Index   191

About the Author   201

Foreword

■ ■ ■

The bulk of this book was written between June 2019 and March 2020, just before the world changed in ways almost no one could have predicted. For most of that time, I was on a sabbatical and had the luxury of time to dedicate to writing, reading, and revising as the book took shape. And then, in March, my time changed just as everyone else's did.

In the early part of the pandemic, like so many others, I spent my days waking up early to work alone, most of the morning supporting my children with their schoolwork, and the afternoons and evenings shuffling in between and wearing more hats at once than anyone ever should. As often as possible throughout that first spring of the pandemic, my children and I explored the outdoors. Playgrounds were closed, and restrictions dictated where and when we could visit. Yet those limitations gave some structure to our journey. Each Tuesday we visited the trails behind a local nature center and watched as eggs hatched into tadpoles and tadpoles became salamanders. We also trekked to the beach once a week or so to play in the cold sand and clean up accumulated trash. On our morning walks around the neighborhood with our dog, we noticed changes in leaves, flowers, and creatures; it is pretty incredible to see how many earthworms are visible after a rainstorm!

I also felt a need to create, perhaps to gain a sense of control. I began with planting seedlings and starting a worm composting bin, then went on to begin a sourdough phase. I registered for an online jewelry-making class. And I wrote, furiously, early in the morning. In the end, I wrote two articles about the everyday science experiences I shared with my children. The act of creating grounded me in this time and made a mark to remember it by.

Throughout that first spring, I kept in close touch with many teachers—friends and colleagues, former students, and the women tasked with teaching my own children. I saw their worry and hopes and the way in which this time shaped their own teaching. Often, through no fault of their own, science went to the back burner. Finding ways to teach science in this online environment was challenging for everyone and something no one was prepared for. My son's first grade teachers took the opportunity to combine science and writing as they challenged the class to create books about animals, then culminated the experience with a virtual trip to visit each child's animal at the San Diego Zoo. A third grade teacher I know walked her students through virtual engineering design challenges during weekly Zoom meetings and had students share their work through Flipgrid videos. YouTube exploded with teachers in lab coats at their kitchen tables growing seedlings and making volcanoes.

As spring changed to summer and schools began making plans for the 2020–2021 academic year, uncertainty was normalized. Schools made plans to return to fully remote learning, hybrid settings that included students in-person and at a distance, and in some cases face-to-face. Children who were able to attend school in person wore masks, sat distanced from classmates, and sometimes had transparent barriers separating them from others. But they all made do.

For my own elementary science teaching methods students, who would be test-driving early versions of the chapters in this book, we were required to use a remote-only format. I created at-home science kits for the future teachers to use in testing out strategies introduced in our class. Though it was surely imperfect, I believe this chance to interact with materials made for meaningful learning experiences.

At first, I thought I might expand the chapters in this book after using it once to teach, and in some cases I did, especially when additional directions or clarifications were necessary. However, the text remains relatively straightforward with simple-to-follow strategies and justifications for using them. As the educational landscape continues to shift and change, the possibility of children sitting in groups working together on experiments becomes easier to envision. Yet teachers—practicing and future—need usable and straightforward ideas right now as they prepare for the unknown in their future classrooms. I am confident that the ideas offered in this book can help teachers to structure meaningful and engaging science learning with a simple and easy-to-use approach.

Acknowledgments

■ ■ ■

There are so many people who helped support the creation of this book. First and foremost, many thanks to Mark Kerr and Courtney Packard at Rowman & Littlefield for their guidance and thoughtful suggestions throughout the entire process. I am especially grateful to have had the opportunity to "test drive" this book before sending it off. The following students provided anonymous feedback on each chapter and helped clarify the writing and approach: Kaitlyn Bannon, Danielle Berson, Christina Cammarata, Erica Cerbasio, Heather Collins, Sophie Connell, Jason Gardner, Taheara Gibson-Clark, Jade Gunshefski, Kelsey Kobus, Stephanie Kravitz, Ashlyn Maclure, Emily Margolin, Jillian Martin, Chris McCormack, Jill Messineo, Jordan Moritz, Nicole Nigro, Carrie Torbick, Justin Valerio, Autumn VanBuskirk, Megan Warker, Nia Watson, and Patrick Wenz.

The following teacher-leaders and STEM supervisors also provided invaluable feedback on each chapter of the book: Helen Corveleyn, Christina Overman, Kristin Burke, and Vicky Pilitsis.

I am also grateful to the anonymous reviewers who provided commentary and suggestions on the first draft of this book.

The College of New Jersey provided me with the time and funding to complete this project while on sabbatical, and I am full of gratitude to work at such a supportive institution. My students, colleagues, and friends at TCNJ's School of Education and beyond were the very best cheerleaders throughout this process. The informal writing groups and sabbatical faculty meetups were much-needed (and appreciated) motivators in completing this project.

My family gave endless support and unconditional love as I took on this project. Special thanks go to my first inspiration and mom, Diane O'Neill. My husband manages to halve my worries and double my joys; Mike Madden, every challenge is easier to face with you by my side. Connor and Luke Madden, you never cease to amaze me. The wonder in your eyes and hearts is enough to spark scientific explorations for the rest of eternity. This book is dedicated to the memory of my dad, Edward O'Neill, whose curiosity always fueled mine.

1

An Introduction to Assets-Based Elementary Science Teaching

■ ■ ■

Imagine a child, six or seven years old, collecting seashells at the beach. After her bucket is full, she sorts the shells by size, color, shape, and type. She carefully studies the nuances of each one and can explain why each shell is unique to her friends and family. She might guess how a shell's shape could influence the role that creature plays in its ecosystem. She might try to figure out which shells are normally found near one another or what other plants and animals can also be found near her favorite shells. To many parents, teachers, and child-care providers, this scene is familiar. And when children engage in this kind of exploration of their worlds, we adults often celebrate this kind of exploration by assuring those curious children that they are *doing science*!

In truth, these patterns continue in our everyday lives in so many ways that we adults often fail to notice. We are definitely *doing science* when we substitute an ingredient in a recipe based on our prior knowledge of similarities and differences in taste, texture, and smell. When we try to figure out how a young pitcher can change his stance to throw a faster curveball, we are *doing science*. And when we remember to fill up our gas tanks early in the morning on hot, sunny days to get the best value for our money, we are certainly *doing science*.

Why is it that when we think about the ways in which we explore the world around us, something changes when those explorations are done by adults rather than children? For some individuals, the idea of doing science changes when in-school instruction moves away from focusing heavily on using observation and exploration to understand the world around us. When complicated vocabulary and heavy mathematical

Figure 1.1 Girls sorting seashells on the beach. (Margaret Martin)

formulas start to define what science is, many people, including teachers, stop recognizing their own scientific interactions in day-to-day life. In this textbook, we will devote much attention to our own scientific interactions and use them to help children explore effectively.

The purpose of this textbook is to create a guide to help teachers and children build scientific literacy, advocate for science, and use science in their day-to-day lives. The book begins with a look at educational theorists and an introduction to inquiry. It moves on to cover what science is and isn't, or the nature of science. Next, it will provide a guide to the Next Generation Science Standards, the framework we use to build science lessons and curricula in the United States. The middle part of the book focuses on strategies for teaching such as asking good questions; integrating literacy and mathematics into science; and using STEM, STEAM, and creativity in science teaching. Later, I emphasize strategies for advocating for science itself and advocating for equity, diversity, and inclusion in STEM. In chapter 11, I address strategies for assessing learning both formatively and summatively. Finally, I wrap up the text with ideas for taking science outside the classroom in chapter 12. Chapter 13 offers closing thoughts on scientific advocacy and suggestions for tying ideas together from across this text.

ADVOCATING FOR SCIENCE

Scientific thinking is critical in so many parts of everyday life, but *knowing science* is equally important for being an engaged citizen and effective teacher. To know science isn't to know everything about science or to have the ability to recite facts and figures about a variety of topics. Rather, it is the ability to know what science *is* and *isn't* and make informed decisions using scientific information. So what *is* science? We will explore ideas around the nature of science, or what science is and isn't, later on in chapter 4 of this text. Yet, at its simplest, science is using data as evidence to explain phenomena.

Scientifically literate citizens can unpack scientific information to help make decisions about their health and well-being. Evaluating scientific information to make decisions about our homes and work provides a multitude of phenomena to consider in our day-to-day lives. For instance, companies and municipalities that provide water to homes and businesses are required to regularly test water and send out warnings or alerts to consumers when anomalies come up such as elevated levels of certain chemicals. This information is free and accessible to the public. Homeowners can read the information provided by their water company and ask questions. For example, one chemical that water companies often test for is benzene, a common additive to gasoline. Consumption of too much benzene could lead to nervous system damage or possibly cancer. On the other hand, there are some things called "nuisance" chemicals like chlorides. These might change the taste or smell of water but are not harmful to human health. The reports on water quality can tell the homeowner whether levels of a multitude of chemicals are within or higher than the acceptable levels. The homeowner can then research the effects of consuming these chemicals and decide whether or not to purchase bottled water. A decision on whether or not to use bottled water might be different based on which chemical was elevated, and using a scientific approach to describe this phenomenon can help a homeowner to make the best decision for his or her health and well-being.

There are also a suite of issues that are sometimes seen as controversial by the public but scientists generally agree on. These include the effectiveness of vaccines and the existence of human-caused climate change. Later on in chapter 4 of this text, I will dig deeper into why these ideas are controversial and how to use science to better understand these sometimes complex issues and phenomena in an informed way.

SCIENCE INSIDE THE ELEMENTARY CLASSROOM

Recently, many states across the US have adopted the Next Generation Science Standards (NGSS) as guidelines for planning curriculum and instruction.[1] Throughout this text, I will refer to the NGSS structure and goals, with an in-depth look at how these standards work in chapter 5. Generally speaking, the NGSS represent a comprehensive philosophy for science teaching that allows teachers and students to engage deeply in doing science, identify connections between and among scientific ideas, and build on prior knowledge. The NGSS use a three-dimensional approach, which includes science content (called Disciplinary Core Ideas), science and engineering practices, and crosscutting concepts (or the ideas that connect across different science disciplines when setting out performance expectations).

An Activity for Teachers

Think about the very best chocolate chip cookie you've ever eaten. What was it like? Chewy or crispy? Dense or light? How do you think the ingredients that went into that cookie influenced the taste, color, and texture?

In this article,[2] the authors describe how modifying ingredients in the classic Nestlé Toll House Cookie Recipe[3] yields major changes. If you can, after reading the article, bake a batch of cookies using the modification

---

1. Some states have adopted the NGSS in their entirety. Others have modified or *adapted* the NGSS, and others still have created their own standards that are influenced by the NGSS as well. The National Science Teaching Association (NSTA) offers a position statement in which it states, "The National Science Teaching Association (NSTA) recommends the adoption and implementation of the Next Generation Science Standards (NGSS; NGSS Lead States 2013) as an effective, research-based approach to accomplish these goals and transform science education." https://www.nsta.org/about/positions/ngss.aspx.

2. https://www.npr.org/sections/thesalt/2014/09/04/345530660/the-science-behind-baking-your-ideal-chocolate-chip-cookie.

3. https://www.verybestbaking.com/recipes/18476/original-nestle-toll-house-chocolate-chip-cookies/.

Figure 1.2 A freshly baked chocolate chip cookie. (Lauren Madden)

that yields your favorite. Use all five of your senses to describe the cookie and jot down those descriptions. If you're unable to bake a batch of cookies, pick one up at a shop or bakery and infer how the ingredients might have influenced the taste.

A fun class activity could be to bake a batch of "control group" cookies using the original recipe and then seeking modified recipe cookie contributions from families or bringing in some cooking tools and ingredients to class for a baking experiment. For an example lesson plan that involves cooking in the classroom, see the supplementary lesson plan on Cookie Chemistry.

Reflecting on Your Exploration

Though it may have seemed like a cooking activity, comparing and contrasting these cookies comprised some serious scientific thinking. Let's consider the NGSS Performance Expectations that this activity began to explore:

> 2-PS1-1: Plan and conduct an investigation to *describe and classify different kinds of materials by their observable properties.*
>
> 2-PS1-2: Analyze data obtained from testing different materials to *determine which materials have the properties that are best suited for an intended purpose.*

At first blush, these performance expectations might seem overwhelming. They both contain science content, practices, and connections to ideas that underlie all scientific domains. They require more than simply learning the scientific facts or jargon related to a particular idea. And, for the most part, they cannot be covered in a single activity, lesson, or class period. But read them again and think carefully about the cookie investigation.

Once again, think about your own ideal chocolate chip cookie. Which version of the cookies from the article come closest to it?

Which parts of these NGSS performance expectations did we address in this activity?

What kinds of activities or questions could a teacher develop to follow up on the cookie activity to ensure her students were able to identify properties of matter in other situations? What about considering which properties were best suited for a certain purpose?

The vision of the NGSS is to ensure all students have a chance to truly engage with science and not simply learn it for learning's sake. Thinking back to the little girl with the seashells early in this chapter, consider how a teacher might expand upon her curiosity and systemic classification to reach better understanding of a bigger scientific goal.

In closing, you have a challenge: spend twenty-four hours logging your daily activities. Next, identify the ways in which you engaged scientifically with the world either through your actions or your thinking. Bring this log back to class, and we will use it to think more deeply about the way in which we all engage with the world around us as scientists.

CHAPTER 1 SUPPLEMENTARY LESSON: COOKIE CHEMISTRY LESSON

Title: Cookie Chemistry
Standards:
NGSS:

2-PS1-1. Plan and conduct an investigation to describe and classify different kinds of materials by their observable properties.
2-PS1-2. Analyze data obtained from testing different materials to determine which materials have the properties that are best suited for an intended purpose.

Learning Objectives and Assessments:

Objectives	Assessments
The students will be able to describe the ways cookies differ based on their ingredients.	The students will complete tables comparing each group's cookies based on their properties.

Materials:
toaster oven
hand mixer
flour
granulated sugar
brown sugar
butter
eggs
vanilla
chocolate chips
baking soda
baking powder
gluten-free flour
corn syrup
salt
bowls
measuring cups
spatulas
pot holders
cookie sheets

Pre-lesson Assignments/Prior Knowledge:
Students will likely have eaten chocolate chip cookies before. Some may also have helped adults bake cookies as well.

Lesson Beginning (10 minutes):

- Instructor will separate students into six groups.
- Instructor will distribute cookies baked using the classic Toll House chocolate chip cookie recipe and copies of the recipe. (See Handout I.)
- Instructor will ask students to use all five senses to observe the cookies and describe any connections between the recipe and their observations (recording on Handout I).

Instructional Plan:
10:00–30:00

- Each group will be assigned one modification to the classic recipe.
  - Replace granulated sugar with brown sugar.
  - Replace brown sugar with granulated sugar.
  - Replace flour with gluten-free (coconut) flour.
  - Replace half the butter with coconut oil.
  - Double the baking soda.
  - Add a third egg.

- Groups will gather necessary materials and begin baking.
  - Students will follow the recipe on Handout I exactly EXCEPT for the modification selected.
  - Students will bake four to six cookies on their baking sheets.
  - *The remaining dough should be stored in a plastic zip-top bag and labeled with the group name and recipe modification.*

30:00–45:00

- Once cookies are baked, groups will complete Handout II observing their cookie and making comparisons to the original cookie.
- Each group will label one sample cookie with their modification and circulate the room observing differences between the cookies, completing the remainder of Handout II.
- Whole class will have a discussion of observations.

45:00–60:00

- Each person will obtain a copy of the following article, "The Science Behind Baking Your Ideal Chocolate Chip Cookie." The teacher will read this article aloud.
- Whole class will have a discussion about how modifying ingredients leads to differences in cookie outcome.

Differentiation:

- The teacher will used mixed-ability groups and assign specific roles to each individual in the group.
- The teacher will make modifications to the lesson/recipe if food allergies exist.
- Handouts include organizational diagrams and charts to help focus students' investigations throughout the class.

Questions:

- How can you use all five senses to observe your cookie?
- What are some of the differences you can see between the cookies?
- How do the properties of the ingredients affect the outcome of the cookie?

Classroom Management:

- Each group member will be given specific duties to complete.
- Teacher will circulate the room throughout the lesson and use proximity to minimize distractions.
- The teacher will remind students of safety rules and procedures throughout class.

Handout I: Cookie Chemistry Lesson
Recipe adapted from: https://www.verybestbaking.com/recipes/18476
/original-nestle-toll-house-chocolate-chip-cookies/#sm.00002ujnp911mf
8ys0o2js3m369ao.

Ingredients	Instructions
2¼ cups all-purpose flour 1 teaspoon baking soda 1 teaspoon salt 1 cup (2 sticks) butter, softened ¾ cup granulated sugar ¾ cup packed brown sugar 1 teaspoon vanilla extract 2 large eggs 2 cups chocolate chips	**PREHEAT** oven to 375° F. **COMBINE** flour, baking soda, and salt in small bowl. Beat butter, granulated sugar, brown sugar, and vanilla extract in large mixer bowl until creamy. Add egg, beating well after each addition. Gradually beat in flour mixture. Stir in chips. Drop by rounded tablespoon onto ungreased baking sheets. **BAKE** for 9 to 11 minutes or until golden brown. Cool on baking sheets for 2 minutes; remove to wire racks to cool completely.

Record your observations of the cookies on the table below:

Sense	Observation
Sight	
Sound	
Smell	
Touch	
Taste	

Describe any connections you can make between the cookie and the recipe:

Handout II: Cookie Chemistry Lesson
Observe your group's cookie, and record observations on the table below:

Sense	Observation
Sight	
Sound	
Smell	
Touch	
Taste	

Compare and contrast the original cookie to your group's cookie using the Venn diagram below:

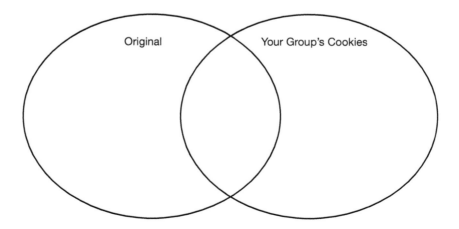

Label your cookie using your modification. Walk around the room and note any differences in the cookies you see. Record your observations on the table below.

Recipe Modification	Observations
• Replace granulated sugar with brown sugar	
• Replace brown sugar with granulated sugar	
• Replace flour with gluten-free flour	
• Replace butter with coconut oil	
• Double the baking soda	
• Add a third egg	

2

A Developmental Perspective on Science Teaching and Learning

■ ■ ■

L ast November, my twin sons turned six. They were in kindergarten and, with the help of their teachers and caretakers, starting to consider their observations of the natural and designed world in a more systematic way. They were ready to observe caterpillars become butterflies and to start playing with motors and Styrofoam pumpkins to create "pumpkin bots" around Halloween.

Figure 2.1 Pumpkin Bots. (Lauren Madden)

Perhaps a bit excited about changes in the toy market since his child-hood, my brother, their uncle, gifted my sons with remote control drones for their birthday. The boys were thrilled. As a family, we waited for a day that wasn't too windy and headed to the park to conduct our first test flight. Before we headed off, I helped them to open the boxes, iden-tify which pieces matched which parts of the diagram, and start to think about drone assembly—only to end up with two very sad and frustrated children. At six, these boys were curious and excited to build something new to play with. But, they also had six-year-old fine motor skills and weren't quite ready to assemble such complicated devices. We turned the boxes over to see the recommended age range for these toys; we learned it was fifteen and over. While no small children like being told they're too young for anything, their sadness was eased a bit with a promise to go to the park anyway—and save these toys for later.

A few months later, my sons were at a doctor's office and saw that the toys there were designed for much younger children and babies. There were many puzzles, but they were designed such that it was sim-ple for a baby or young toddler to see how the shape of the puzzle piece fit into the bigger picture. Though my sons were willing to give these old familiar objects a try again while sitting in the waiting room, they ended up ignoring them and declaring boredom as we waited for their appointments to begin.

In this chapter, we will briefly review ideas related to child development and how to create developmentally appropriate science learning experi-ences for children. The key ideas from educational theorists John Dewey, Jean Piaget, and Lev Vygotsky will help situate our exploration of child development and science learning.

In both situations described above, it was clear that the toys my children engaged with were not the best choices given their age. Though these were toys and generally "low stakes" interactions for my children, they tell a cautionary tale for teachers. In order for children to truly engage in a meaningful learning experience, the experience must be developmen-tally appropriate. This is especially true in science teaching. Science, as a discipline, is full of complexities that can lead to confusion. Introduc-ing mathematical representations before students are ready or discuss-ing things or ideas that occur at scales too large, small, fast, or slow to observe in a class period could frustrate, confuse, or simply turn a student off of science. On the other hand, children enter our classrooms as curious observers and participants in the happenings of our natural and designed worlds. In this chapter, we will consider various educational theorists' perspectives on child development with respect to science teaching.

The seminal National Research Council book *Taking Science to School* (2007) summarizes the state of the research literature on how what we know about child development can inform best practices in science teaching. Several key takeaways about the ways children engage in science include:

- Concern for explanation and causal relationships are central to children's scientific explorations, yet there is no clear path from concrete to abstract representation for children.

  ○ This suggests that teachers should encourage exploration, especially with regard to cause and effect, and help provide guidance for children to make connections between their observations and the abstract ideas that underlie them.

- Children's explanations are domain[1]-specific, and certain domains (e.g., mechanics and folk biology) hold privileged status. These explanations should be built upon or challenged through exploration rather than refuted in science teaching.

  ○ This suggests that teachers should allow children to share their experiences and understandings of the world while also providing opportunities to connect single examples to broader concepts. The NGSS crosscutting concepts provide frameworks for making these connections, which will be discussed later in this book.

- There are patterns of cognitive skills that cut across scientific domains for children. These should be considered when connecting ideas to one another.

  ○ This suggests that teachers should help children notice they are thinking about and engaging in science. The science and engineering practices within the NGSS can help teachers to structure their instruction to help children identify and notice their own scientific interactions.

In this chapter, we will dig a bit deeper and consider the works of three key educational theorists: John Dewey, Jean Piaget, and Lev Vygotsky.

---

1. Domain refers to a field or branch in science in this case. In the Next Generation Science Standards, the term *discipline* or *scientific discipline* is used rather than domain.

We will offer suggestions for how these works can inform guidelines for effective science teaching and learning in the elementary years.

JOHN DEWEY (1859–1952)

Ideas are worthless except as they pass into actions which rearrange and reconstruct in some way, be it little or large, the world in which we live.

—John Dewey, *The Question for Certainty*

Dewey is perhaps known best for his development of the idea of a *progressive education* that focuses on student-centered teaching practices in which students often create and develop their own explanations of the phenomena in the world around them (Wong et al., 2001). The goal of a progressive education is to develop curious lifelong learners rather than students who can cite factual information and engage in rote or formulaic activities. Along those lines, education should include "everyday" knowledge such as cooking and household activities along with more traditional school subjects like science and mathematics. Though his work in education was not exclusive to science alone, Dewey's views can help shape the way we plan science teaching and learning.

In Dewey's vision, students must *experience* in order to have meaningful learning. However, this notion of experience does not mean just "doing." Rather, it refers to purposeful experience, or well-planned activities in which students truly interact with ideas, objects, and the environment around them. As Wong et al. (2001) noted, "The educative experience is evoked, it emerges from the participation of students with the environment as they create and become involved with the drama of its plot" (p. 322). The emphasis here is on children actively participating, rather than simply following a teacher's or textbook's plan for learning. Dewey also believed that the act of doing must be connected with content matter. This notion is especially important for science teaching and learning: science content should not be separated from the practice or act of doing science. For example, sometimes in autumn, early in the school year, a teacher will hold an apple taste test in which children try several different kinds of apples and report their favorite. While this activity is good to help students learn how to collect and record data, it doesn't connect to any bigger science concepts. If instead, the teacher asked students to explore some bigger questions like, "Why are some apples more tart than others?" or "Why do certain types of apples ripen earlier than others?" the students would have an opportunity to consider both the process and content of science through data collection and analysis and engaging in research from authentic scientific texts.

Dewey also emphasized that simple engagement or experience with ideas and concepts was not sufficient. In his view, reflection on those ideas, or "continual reorganization, reconstruction and transformation of experience" (Dewey, 1916, p. 50), is the way in which people learn best. This belief is extremely important for planning science activities. Once children engage with a phenomenon, they need time to talk about it, think about it, and engage with the idea reflectively to truly understand.

Implications for Science Teaching

We can use Dewey's work to help shape science learning experiences in a few clear ways:

1. Allow children to express their own understanding for phenomena they observe.
2. Avoid rote or formulaic activities.
3. Integrate content and process when teaching.
4. Include time for reflection and reorganization of ideas at the conclusion of learning experiences.

Challenge: Imagine you were working on a mealworm investigation with kindergarteners. How might Dewey suggest you help your students determine whether the mealworms prefer wet or dry environments?

Figure 2.2 Children engage in an experiment to determine whether mealworms prefer wet or dry environments. (Jillian Bershtein)

JEAN PIAGET (1896–1980)

I am a constructivist. I think that knowledge is a matter of constant, new construction, by its interaction with reality, and that it is not pre-formed. There is a continuous creativity.

—Jean Piaget, University of Geneva Archives

When asked to think about Piaget's work, teachers often cite two foundational ideas: the idea that children construct knowledge through observation and interaction with the world around them, or **constructivism**, and the idea that development occurs in predictable stages (Piaget, 1964).

Piaget uses the idea of **schema** or mind maps to describe the way in which ideas are organized. When individuals encounter new information, they must either add the new idea to the existing schema through a process called **assimilation** or adjust and reorganize the original schema through a process called **accommodation**. (See figure 2.3.)

According to Piaget, as individuals engage with and experience the world, they continually construct their own organizational systems for this knowledge. The interaction with other people, things, and the environment is critical for developing an understanding. However, the way in which one operates in and interacts with the world changes as one ages and develops. Piaget uses four categories to define these operational stages, as described in table 2.1.

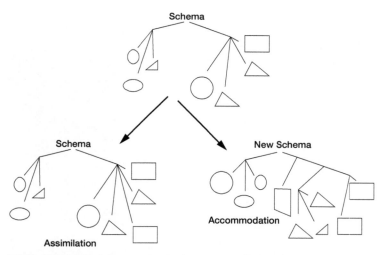

Figure 2.3 Pigetian assimilation and accommodation in schema.

Table 2.1

Stage	Characterized by
Sensory-Motor: *Piaget used birth to eighteen months of age to categorize this time frame.*	Young children who are pre-verbal perceive and interact with what they can see in their immediate environment. Young babies cannot perceive things they cannot see (object permanence). Toward the end of this phase, children begin to perceive sequence and causality.
Pre-Operational *Piaget used ages two to seven to categorize this time frame.*	Children in this phase are beginning to use language and symbols. Children do not yet reverse operations or understand conservation of volume or quantity. Children are highly egocentric at this stage.
Concrete Operational *Piaget used ages seven to eleven to characterize this time frame.*	Children in this phase can use logic and order to organize thoughts and ideas. Children can begin to see reversibility and understand that manipulating space and arrangement does not necessarily affect conservation. Egocentrism begins to diminish at this phase.
Formal or Hypothetical Operational *Piaget used age eleven to adulthood to characterize this time frame.*	Children and teens in this phase can use models, logic, and abstraction to interpret the world. Hypothetical thinking and proportional reasoning are used.

Piaget argued that there are four main factors that influence development from one phase to the next: age or maturation, experience in the world, social transmission (e.g., through education or language), and finally equilibration (Piaget, 1964). Though many have found that the age ranges Piaget suggests for each phase might not hold true across time and location, these developmental markers must occur in order to move from simply observing the world to interacting with it, representing it, and thinking abstractly.

Implications for Science Teaching

Piaget's work carefully considers the way in which children develop as learners and can be used to guide the way science experiences are crafted and shaped. For example:

1. Be aware of children's prior knowledge and experiences when planning learning.
2. Encourage interaction with materials in the classroom and nature, specifically with concrete objects whenever possible.
3. Provide opportunities for children to interact with one another.
4. Consider phases of development when selecting materials and activities for the classroom.

Challenge: Imagine you are working with third graders just beginning to explore electric circuits using batteries, bulbs, and wires. How might Piaget suggest you introduce the topic?

> Mr. Jones, a second grade teacher, asked his students to measure out 50 mL of water before starting an activity in which students tested which powders would dissolve in water. Short on materials, he gathered as many graduated cylinders as he could. Some held 50 mL, some held 100 mL, and some held 200 mL. He paired his students and asked them to begin measuring.
>
> One pair of students with a 200 mL graduated cylinder asked for help. They thought their container had less water than their neighbors, who were using a 50 mL graduated cylinder. When Mr. Jones looked at the students' work, he saw that the first pair had water that went about a quarter of the way up the cylinder while the second pair had a cylinder that was nearly full. What advice might you give to Mr. Jones in this situation?

LEV VYGOTSKY (1896–1934)

What lies in the zone of proximal development at one stage is realized and moves to the level of actual development at a second. In other words, what the child is able to do in collaboration today he will be able to do independently tomorrow.

—Lev Vygotsky, *Thinking and Speech*

Vygotsky saw learning as a social act and is best known for his ideas about collaboration in learning, or the notion that knowledge is constructed socially, *social constructivism* (Wells, 1994). Vygotsky's work focused on learning in general, as well as learning about science concepts in particular. With regard to learning scientific concepts, Vygotsky defined these as ideas that have systemic features, rather than simple observations of the world around us or general observations (Wells, 1994). These scientific concepts require a set of terms and symbols to allow others to discuss them. For example, terms like "atom" and "molecule" can help adults to engage in a conversation about matter.

When considering the way people learn new information, Vygotsky recognized the importance of *tools*, with language being the most important tool of all (Wells, 1994). By using tools, both physical and through the use of symbols or language, individuals can share ideas and discuss a concept together. Language and symbols are the way in which adults transmit knowledge to children, and children then take those ideas and build upon them. Vygotsky emphasized the importance of engaging with language through internal dialogue (thinking), dialogue with others (talking), or recording dialogue (writing) as they develop understanding. These suggestions emphasize the importance of allowing children to talk about science using everyday language independently and with peers before formal scientific vocabulary is introduced. Returning to the example of matter, children should be able to express their own understanding of matter in their own words before the more formal terms are introduced.

Perhaps Vygotsky is best known for his idea of the *Zone of Proximal Development (ZPD)*. This is often described as the space between what an individual can accomplish on her own and what she can do with the assistance of another, more able peer, teacher, or parent (Wells, 1994).

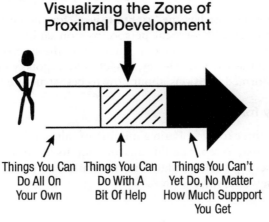

Visualizing the Zone of Proximal Development

Things You Can Do All On Your Own

Things You Can Do With A Bit Of Help

Things You Can't Yet Do, No Matter How Much Suppport You Get

Figure 2.4 Visual representation of Vygotsky's Zone of Proximal Development.

Scaffolding is a process that occurs when a teacher structures an activity such that a student is able to work within the ZPD and better able to reach the intended learning goal. It should be noted, however, that scaffolds can include physical tools, such as information sheets or guides, or simple instructions from a more able peer to help a child meet his or her own learning goals. This concept suggests that mixed-ability groups can help children to learn science effectively within their own ZPD. Similarly *apprenticeship* is the process by which children can shadow or work alongside more able peers or adults to learn a new concept.

Implications for Science Teaching

Vygotsky's work helps us to think about the ways in which people learn about new ideas and how teachers can structure learning experiences. Some key takeaways include:

1. Structure groups so that children can interact with tools and language collaboratively.
2. Create activities that allow children time to internalize their thoughts before sharing them with others or using scientific names.
3. Allow children to interact with more able peers.

Challenge: Imagine you're working with a class of fifth graders building towers out of rolled-up paper. Some children in your class have a lot of experience building with Lego bricks and other toys, but others do not. How would Vygotsky suggest you set up groups to best facilitate learning?

PUTTING THE PIECES TOGETHER

While no one theorist has the "right answer" for the best way to teach science, considering theoretical perspectives on child development can help us ensure that we meet our students at the appropriate starting point. Taking the work of Dewey, Piaget, and Vygotsky collectively, we can make informed decisions about how to best structure lessons.

An Activity for Teachers

In groups of three to five, obtain a mixture of salt, sand, and cotton. Your challenge is, first, to separate this mixture into its three component parts. You may use any tools available in the classroom (which should have coffee filters, water, stirrers, etc.).

Next, consider the works of Dewey, Piaget, and Vygotsky. Create a table to describe how each theorist's ideas could be used to create structure for this activity.

Table 2.2

Suggestions based on Dewey's ideas	Suggestions based on Piaget's ideas	Suggestions based on Vygotsky's ideas

Finally, remember the NGSS Standards introduced in the Cookie Chemistry activity in chapter 1 of this book. In this activity, readers were encouraged to make modifications to a classic cookie recipe in order to understand how these changes in recipe reflect the outcome.

2-PS1-1: Plan and conduct an investigation to *describe and classify different kinds of materials by their observable properties.*

2-PS1-2: Analyze data obtained from testing different materials to *determine which materials have the properties that are best suited for an intended purpose.*

Considering the mixture separation activity in light of theory on child development, how might you sequence the two lessons—Cookie Chemistry and Mixture Separation—to best facilitate children's learning about properties of materials?

CONCLUSION

In summary, understanding our students from a developmental perspective allows us to create meaningful learning experiences suited to their needs. Dewey, Piaget, and Vygotsky each offer theories that can be helpful for framing our work to align well with children's developmental levels.

3

Inquiry-Based Teaching

Connecting Theory to Strategy

■ ■ ■

The scientist is not a person who gives the right answers; he's one who asks the right questions.

—Claude Lévi-Strauss, French anthropologist

If a prospective teacher were to scroll through Pinterest or Teachers Pay Teachers looking for ideas for how to teach science, it wouldn't be long before she came across lessons that were labeled "inquiry-based." At the most basic level, inquiry-based science simply means science that starts with a question. In this chapter, we will explore foundations of inquiry-based science teaching, consider several models for inquiry-based science teaching, and consider some examples and counterexamples of learning science through inquiry.

This chapter will provide an overview of inquiry-based science teaching. We will look at some models for different types of inquiry and follow up with the history of inquiry in the United States. Finally, several strategies for inquiry-based instruction, including the 5E Learning Cycle and discrepant events, will be introduced.

The National Science Teaching Association (NSTA) is the US professional organization for science teachers. NSTA offers position statements about best practices, ideas, and skills important for science teaching and learning. In one position statement, the NSTA suggests that understanding scientific inquiry requires both knowledge and skill and should be seen as a "habit of the mind" or way of thinking (NSTA, 2018b). In order to engage completely in inquiry, the NSTA suggests using a three-dimensional learning approach, in line with the ideas set forth in the Next Generation Science Standards and Framework for K–12 Science Education. These ideas will be expanded upon further in chapter 5 of this text. But first, we'll explore what we mean by inquiry-based science teaching.

AN EXAMPLE ACTIVITY

Consider the following question: Which will melt first, an ice cube in a cup of freshwater or an ice cube in a cup of saltwater? Why did you choose that answer?

Make sure to record your response and reasoning, and gather the following materials: two empty cups, water, salt, and two ice cubes of approximately the same size. Follow the procedure below.

1. Fill the cups to the same level, about 8 fluid ounces.
2. Label one cup "freshwater" and the other "saltwater." Add 1 teaspoon of salt to the saltwater cup and stir.
3. Observe the ice cubes melting and record your observation using pictures and words until both cubes have melted completely.

Once the ice cubes have melted, return to the guiding question above. Did the experiment support or refute your original claim? How? What might the next steps be to better understand why the faster melting cube melted first?

Figure 3.1 Ice cubes in fresh and saltwater. (Lauren Madden)

Were you surprised to see the outcome of the experiment? Why do you think the cube melted first? With a group of classmates, design a way to figure out why this occurred. We will return to this activity in the future.

INQUIRY-BASED SCIENCE INSTRUCTION

The melting ice cube activity was an example of a *scientific inquiry*, or an activity that starts with a question. This investigation asked the learner to draw on prior knowledge and everyday observation of ice cubes in order to make a prediction about the outcome. Yet the ice cube activity included no specialized scientific tools, equipment, or handouts that one might find on Pinterest or Teachers Pay Teachers. The idea of learning through inquiry can be simple and straightforward and draw on everyday knowledge and experiences. Yet, when we observe science lessons or reflect on our own science learning experiences, they're often more like the Montillation of Traxoline than like the ice cube activity.

In this example, a student can read the paragraph full of nonsense words yet still answer the questions given by simply repeating what is stated in the passage above. Where is traxoline montilled? Traxoline is montilled in Ceristanna. These words have no meaning, yet the right answer is obvious because it is provided for the student in the passage. In an inquiry-based approach to teaching and learning, children should not be able to answer questions without observing, exploring, and engaging with ideas and phenomena.

The Montillation of Traxoline

It is very important that you learn about traxoline. Traxoline is a new form of zionter. It is montilled in Ceristanna. The Ceristannians gristeriate large amounts of fevon and then bracter it to quasel traxoline. Traxoline may well be one of our most lukized snezlaus in the future because of our zionter lescelidge.

1. What is traxoline?

2. Where is traxoline montilled?

3. How is traxoline quaselled?

4. Why is it important to know about traxoline?

Figure 3.2 The Montillation of Traxoline.

Sometimes, in science and other academic disciplines considered to be challenging, teachers make a decision to focus on *telling* or defining ideas and concepts rather than allowing students to question and explore and come to their own conclusions. In a classroom, this *telling* might look like reading a passage and responding to questions as in the example above, watching a film, or simply copying notes given by the teacher. As a result, students simply recall or repeat information rather than building understanding. This type of instruction also often includes ***confirmatory*** laboratories or investigations. Confirmatory investigations start by providing students with explanations of phenomena or patterns. Next, the students follow a prescribed procedure to confirm the explanation they were given. For example, high school chemistry students often learn the difference between exothermic and endothermic reactions by memorizing examples and drawing diagrams of the step-by-step process for each type of example. Students in this example might first be told that exothermic reactions release heat and get warmer and would then follow a lab procedure to combine two substances that react exothermically and observe the change in temperature. This activity simply confirms what the students have already learned. How might the students' experience differ if the activities were switched? What if they were to follow a lab procedure in which they combined two substances and found they released heat? Then, the teacher could follow up with a reading or lecture to help students make sense of their observations.

The Continuum of Inquiry

Though confirmatory science instruction can be simple to identify and describe, inquiry-based science teaching can take a multitude of formats. Banchi and Bell (2008) provide a simple, straightforward framework for categorizing science instruction across a spectrum of strategies as depicted in figure 3.3 below.

The Continuum of Inquiry

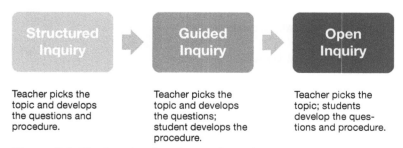

Figure 3.3 The Inquiry Continuum based on Banchi and Bell's (2008) model.

Though Banchi and Bell's original work includes confirmation inquiry as a first step, from the perspective of this textbook, confirmatory activities are not inquiry-based. The next step in that continuum is *structured inquiry* in which the teacher selects the topic and develops the questions and procedure. The first part of the ice cube experiment in which the students investigate the teacher's question and follow the procedure as written is an example of a structured inquiry investigation. The next level of Banchi and Bell's model is *guided inquiry* in which the teacher selects the topic and develops the questions, but the students design the procedure. The second part of the ice cube experiment in which students develop procedures to test and explain why the cubes melted in the order they did is an example of a guided inquiry investigation. *Open inquiries* are ones in which the students develop the questions *and* procedure, while the teacher selects the overall topic. Later in this textbook, we'll encounter examples of open inquiries that could be used to engage learners across the K–6 spectrum.

In Mrs. Best's fifth grade class, students were exploring weathering and erosion to address the following NGSS performance expectation:

5-ESS2-1. Develop a model using an example to describe ways the geosphere, biosphere, hydrosphere, and/or atmosphere interact.

The students used stream tables or paint trays full of sand, silt, clay, and cocoa powder (to represent the finest-grain size particles we sometimes see in landforms) to model Earth's surface and plastic cups with holes on the bottom to pour water through to model rain. They were experimenting to determine how the slope of the table and size of the water hole influenced the size, path, and speed of the stream formed on their table. One student asked, "What if we used a really big hole and a really high slope?" Mrs. Best changed plans and asked the whole class to gather around that student's table so they could all see the way in which changing multiple variables affected the outcome. This is an example of shifting instruction from guided to open inquiry within the space of a specific lesson.

It should be clear, though, that across all these levels of inquiry, it is not necessary to use *"the"* scientific method. In fact, there is no one scientific method, not even the one that you memorized in middle school and that might have started each science course throughout your secondary education. Scientists use many methods and strategies in their work. Later on, in chapter 4 of this text, we will further investigate the nature of science, or what science *is* and *isn't*.

Foundations for Inquiry-Based Science

Considering that the inquiry-based approach to science teaching might seem different from what you experienced as a learner, you may be surprised to know that inquiry has been the preferred and recommended approach to science teaching for more than a century. Think back to the theorists covered in chapter 2 of this text. Beginning in the 1920s, Dewey made suggestions for science teaching that included building upon children's prior experiences interacting in the natural world and reflecting on those experiences in order to make sense of their observations. He also suggested that teachers integrate content and practice and not teach the act of doing science separately from the science content itself. Similarly, Piaget emphasized the importance of building on prior knowledge and allowing students to interact with materials and one another.

In *A History of Ideas in Science Education*, George DeBoer details a long history of emphasizing inquiry-based instruction in the United States. In the 1950s, during the Cold War, the US and the Soviet Union were embroiled in a space race, a competition to enhance aerospace capabilities with an end goal of sending humans to space. This space race made excellence in science and engineering a priority for our nation and resulted in increased emphasis on science and mathematics education. Science teachers across the US were encouraged to cease using confirmatory investigations in their classrooms and begin encouraging students to truly engage in authentic inquiry-based science. By the early 1980s, the federal government began funding research and development around inquiry-based science materials as kits that were ready-to-use in elementary classrooms including lesson plans, tools, and materials packaged in class sets. Many of these kits, created by companies such as FOSS (Full Option Science Systems), are still widely used in elementary classrooms across the US today.

But Why Inquiry?

Despite the fact that inquiry-based science teaching applies best practices suggested by theorists and has been viewed by many—from educational researchers to the federal government—as the preferred path for science instruction, it still often takes a back seat to confirmatory instruction. Inquiry-based science teaching can result in students developing a more comprehensive understanding of *science concepts* rather than a rote recall of scientific facts and figures. As Konicek-Moran and Keeley (2015) note:

> In science, we use fundamental building blocks of thought that have depth and call them concepts. Words, such as energy, force, evaporation, respiration, heat, erosion, and acceleration, are labels for concepts. They are abstractions developed in the minds of people who tried to understand what was happening in their world. Concepts may also consist of more than one word or a short phrase such as conservation of energy, balanced and unbalanced forces, food chain, or closed system. Concepts imply meaning behind natural phenomena such as phases of the Moon, transfer of energy, condensation, or cell division. (p. 5)

Once achieved, conceptual understanding of fundamental scientific ideas can help students to explain observations, construct connections between ideas, and interact with the world in a more scientific way. This video[1] does a nice job summing up why conceptual understanding is important in science.

Brunsell (2010) echoes these sentiments about conceptual understanding and starting scientific investigations with questions and offers some suggestions about inquiry that emphasize evidence. He offers that there are five components to inquiry-based teaching:

- Learner engages in scientifically oriented questions.
- Learner gives priority to evidence in responding to questions.
- Learner formulates explanations from evidence.
- Learner connects explanations to scientific knowledge.
- Learner communicates and justifies explanations.

This emphasis on evidence and explanation requires the student or learner to reflect on observations to use data as evidence in order to create scientific explanation.

STRATEGIES FOR INQUIRY-BASED SCIENCE TEACHING

Just as there are many ways to think about inquiry-based science, there are many strategies teachers can employ to plan and execute inquiry-based instruction.

---

1. "Conceptual Understanding in Science," https://www.youtube.com/watch?v=3xv Y20jtjr0.

Learning Cycle Models for Inquiry-Based Science Teaching

In the 1960s, Atkin and Karplus (1962) advocated for a "learning cycle" model for instruction. This learning cycle included a phase in which students were able to explore phenomena, followed by defining terms and explaining concepts, and concluding with an application of scientific concepts. This work was well received, and extensive research supported its effectiveness in helping children to develop conceptual understanding of scientific ideas.

Perhaps the most well-recognized model for inquiry-based instruction is the 5E Learning Cycle Model. Developed by Richard Bybee in 1987 through the Biological Sciences Curriculum Study, this model builds upon Atkin and Karplus's original model as depicted in figure 3.4.

Figure 3.4 The 5E Learning Cycle Model, based on Bybee (1987).

Engage

The first part of the 5E Learning Cycle, Engage, is when the teacher learns about what the students might already know about a given topic. There could be questioning, open exploration, or other short activities in which students begin to become more curious about the topic. This is sometimes thought of as a "hook" to get students excited about learning.

Explore

During this second phase, students interact with materials, communicate with peers, and have concrete learning experiences about a given topic.

This could include confronting some misconceptions or following a more prescribed procedure. As Duran and Duran (2004) note, this phase "provides the students with a common, concrete learning experience."

Explain

During the explain phase, the teacher builds upon the students' prior exploration to begin the sense-making process regarding the scientific explanation of phenomena. As Bybee (2014) says, "Using students' explanations and experiences, the teacher introduces scientific or technological concepts briefly and explicitly." The explanation phase is typically verbal or written but could also include other media sources such as videos or diagrams.

Extend

The students develop a deeper understanding of scientific phenomena during this phase. The purpose of this phase is to connect the current phenomenon of interest to students' prior knowledge and experiences, apply knowledge to new contexts, or even make connections to other disciplines. This phase often includes integration of technology.

Evaluate

Teachers check students' progress during the evaluate phase of the 5E Learning Cycle. This can also include students' peer or self-assessments. Evaluation can include formal and informal assessment, ranging from simple observations of students' notes to more formalized homework assignments or quizzes. The goal of this section is for teachers to use evidence to determine how well the students have mastered the content.

The 5E Learning Cycle model can be quite flexible. It is possible to run through all five phases in a single class period or expand them across a longer learning experience. Since it was first introduced in 1987, teachers and researchers have applied this model to other content areas, such as social studies. Still others have expanded upon the model. For example, Eisenkraft (2003) suggests including an "Elicit prior understanding" phase before *Engage* and including an *Elaborate* phase after learning has been evaluated.

Phases of Inquiry Model

Sometimes it is valuable to think about inquiry-based instruction using a more simplistic cycle. In some earlier work looking at the way students represent scientific ideas graphically, we considered three phases: pre-, during-, and post-inquiry (Madden & Wiebe, 2013). In this model, all activities that come prior to engaging with a phenomena, such as gathering materials, asking questions, and making predictions, are part of the "pre-inquiry" phase. Manipulating materials, conducting experiments, observing, and recording data are the "during-inquiry" phase. Finally, making sense of observations, connecting observations to predictions, making conclusions, and revising initial ideas fall into the "post-inquiry" phase. This model is not necessarily in conflict with the 5E model but could be used to think about investigations differently.

Discrepant Events

Another simple strategy for engaging students with scientific inquiry is to use discrepant events. Discrepant events are short demonstrations that showcase the science behind everyday phenomena and spark cognitive dissonance in the observers that often results in motivating learners to explore the idea further. They are short, simple, and engaging hooks to invite the learner into science. Common discrepant events include creating a "disappearing glass" as shown in this video[2] to understand the way different liquids influence the way light moves through transparent objects. This sort of activity could precede instruction on properties of matter or nutrition, depending on how a teacher chose to implement it. Another common example of a discrepant event teachers like to use is a "cloud in a bottle" such as the example shown in this video[3] to explain cloud formation. These activities are pre-inquiry activities and also fit well in the *Engage* phase of the 5E cycle.

Challenge: take some time to think about scientific topics that might have confused you or seemed boring when you were in elementary school. Research some discrepant events related to those phenomena and think about how you might introduce the topic differently as a teacher. For example, if refraction and reflection of light were confusing, are there demonstrations using mirrors and lights that you think could have helped? Why or why not?

Is Inquiry the Only Way?

Across the board, inquiry-based science instruction is well regarded as the preferred path for science instruction. Yet often confirmatory instruction and rote memorization take place instead. Is there ever a time when it is preferred to *not* use an inquiry-based approach?

2. "Disappearing Glass Discrepant Event," https://www.youtube.com/watch?v=tiB-g U0W-OA.
3. "Cloud in a Bottle Discrepant Event," https://www.youtube.com/watch?v=H1dQ8 AipCWI.

The short answer is yes. The first example that comes to mind is safety. Children should never discover that electrocution is dangerous or that broken glass can cut their skin. If the scientific phenomena to be explored include features that might be harmful or unsafe for children, then teacher-driven modeling or simply "telling" might be the preferred instructional methodology. There are also some things that are impossible for children to interact with within the space of a classroom. For example, when studying geologic time, children cannot engage directly with a phenomenon. In that case, technologically driven simulations or physical models might provide a good alternative. The same is true with objects that are too small to be seen in the context of a typical elementary school classroom. In this case, viewing diagrams can replace hands-on investigations. On the other end of the spectrum, exploring planetary objects might also be impossible, and excellent diagrams, readings, and storytelling can help students make sense of the phenomena. Using models, storytelling, and scientific argumentation and debate are all well-regarded strategies for engaging children with science that don't follow an inquiry-based approach yet support the notion that children must explore and interact with objects and ideas.

CONCLUSION

Inquiry-based science instruction can look many different ways in different classrooms but should always include several key attributes: starting with a question, allowing students to explore phenomena, building on prior knowledge, and using evidence to construct scientific explanations.

As a challenge, consider the performance expectation for fifth graders from the NGSS below and create a short outline describing how you could use an inquiry-based approach to address this standard.

> 5-PS1-2. Measure and graph quantities to provide evidence that regardless of the type of change that occurs when heating, cooling, or mixing substances, the total weight of matter is conserved.

What kinds of materials would you use? What sort of changes would you ask the students to examine? How much guidance would you offer the students when conducting their investigation?

4

What Is (and Isn't)
Science Anyway?

■ ■ ■

Science is a way of thinking much more than it is a body of knowledge.

—Carl Sagan

In this chapter we will discuss science as an epistemology, or way of knowing the world. We will unpack ideas related to the nature of science (NOS), which helps to describe and categorize what is and isn't science.

When I hear someone say, "I don't believe in climate change," my immediate response is, "Me either!" This isn't because I disagree with the scientific consensus or enormous body of evidence supporting the idea that our climate is warming more rapidly than ever before in history. It is because science is not about belief.

You may recall science courses in the past that started with a unit on *The Scientific Method*. During those units, you probably memorized a series of steps: question, hypothesis, experiment, results, and conclusion. And though there are many cases in which this process plays out in scientific enterprise, it is far from the only method used by scientists in their work. As Thurs (2015) notes, when we reduce science to one simple method or formula, "we deprive ourselves of a richer perspective in favor of one both narrow and contrary to the way things actually are." Consider the work of a scientist whose research is exploratory rather than experimental: how could you create an experiment to test star formation or the discovery of new bacteria?

Rather than relying on one catchall method, science is more like a process of better understanding how the world works. NASA's *Space Place* website states: "Science consists of observing the world by watching, listening, observing, and recording. Science is curiosity in thoughtful action about the world and how it behaves" (Erickson, 2019). Science is often thought of as an ***epistemology***, or way that one can know or understand the world. Some might wonder: is it possible to be a scientist and religious? And the answer is a resounding yes. Throughout history, many of the world's most famous scientists also held deep religious beliefs, from Gregor Mendel, an Augustinian monk famous for studying heredity in pea plants and known as the father of genetics, to Rosalind Franklin, the British chemist, X-ray crystallographer, and devout practitioner of Judaism whose work helped us to understand the structure of DNA. Brother Guy Consalmango is the Vatican's chief astronomer. He was interviewed about his religious beliefs and scientific understandings and responded as such: "Astronomy is a great way to use science to introduce people to the idea that the universe is bigger than what's for lunch, that there's more to life than your immediate day-to-day needs. And that's what religion tries to do, as well" (Bell, 2017).

Yet it should be clear that when we plan science instruction, our focus is on science explicitly. And in order to do so, teachers need to be prepared to address the nature of science with their students to ensure that they know what science *is* and *isn't*. According to the Understanding Evolution group, a partnership between the University of California Museum of Paleontology (UCMP) and the National Center for Science Education, there are three basic questions of science (Understanding Evolution, n.d.):

- *What is there?*
  This question is useful in many contexts from understanding which organelles exist within a cell to what the atmosphere is like on a new planet.

- *How does it work?*
  Tracking the path of electrons in a circuit or determining the mechanism for digestion can fit underneath this broad question.

- *How did it come to be this way?*
  When scientists study the histories of objects of all kinds, they examine this question. For example, studying the chemical composition of an ice core can help scientists to understand the atmospheric composition at a given point in time.

At the most basic level, scientific investigations explore one or more of these three questions. When we delve further into our investigations of what science is, we can start to consider the nature of science (NOS). The National Science Teaching Association offers a position statement on the NOS, and its preamble is as follows:

> All those involved with science teaching and learning should have a common, accurate view of the nature of science. Science is characterized by the systematic gathering of information through various forms of direct and indirect observations and the testing of this information by methods including, but not limited to, experimentation. The principal product of science is knowledge in the form of naturalistic concepts and the laws and theories related to those concepts.

A few years back, I was teaching an elementary science teaching methods course. Groups of students (preservice teachers) shared examples of discrepant events. One group selected an activity in which they dissolved polystyrene packing peanuts in acetone. When it came time to clean up, the students noticed that the plastic measuring cup they used to hold the acetone had begun to turn to liquid and drip from the bottom. This led the class to brainstorm about the phenomenon and me, as the teacher, to change course in my plans for the next few weeks.

I asked each group of three to four students in class to come up with a question related to the plastic and acetone phenomenon. Next, they made predictions and designed procedures to explore their questions. Over the next few weeks, we dedicated part of our class time to continuing these explorations until we learned more about the phenomenon. A few weeks in, one group, testing rubbing alcohol, vinegar, and acetone in different concentrations for reaction with plastic measuring cups, noticed that some liquids evaporated. A group member suggested adding more liquid and covering the containers. We stopped right there and had a whole group discussion about the practice of science and importance of systematically following procedures to the end. This was a meaningful opportunity to really consider what science is and how it works for the whole class—teacher and students alike.

The Next Generation Science Standards (NGSS) connect each standard to characteristics of NOS in appendix H. These characteristics, which have been consistent throughout the NGSS and earlier documents such as the *Benchmarks for Science Literacy* and the *National Science Education Standards*, are as follows:

- Scientific investigations use a variety of methods.
- Scientific knowledge is based on empirical evidence.
- Scientific knowledge is open to revision in light of new evidence.
- Scientific models, laws, mechanisms, and theories explain natural phenomena.
- Science is a way of knowing.
- Scientific knowledge assumes an order and consistency in natural systems.
- Science is a human endeavor.
- Science addresses questions about the natural and material world.

The NGSS separate these eight ideas into two categories: the first four are most closely related to the science and engineering practices within the NGSS and the last four are most closely related to the crosscutting concepts. In chapter 5 of this text, we will explore the various components of the NGSS, but the practices are simply the things that scientists and engineers do in their work while the crosscutting concepts are overarching ideas that connect across scientific disciplines. Below, we will unpack some specific guidance around each of these eight ideas.

SCIENTIFIC INVESTIGATIONS USE A VARIETY OF METHODS

As noted earlier, there is no one scientific method. Rather, scientists use many strategies to better understand the way the world works. Pose a few scientific questions related to your own school context to your students and challenge them to think of how you might go about investigating them. For example, students could explore the types of rocks found in your school yard, measure rainfall at different doors around the school, or determine the number of days it takes for the leaves to fall off trees visible from a classroom window. All of these questions are scientific ways to engage within your own school, but they each require a different type of experiment or plan to measure their results.

SCIENTIFIC KNOWLEDGE IS
BASED ON EMPIRICAL EVIDENCE

Empirical evidence is simply data that were observed or measured directly being used to support or refute a claim. At the earliest age, the NGSS require students to look for patterns and order in observations in order to create explanations or make arguments about scientific knowledge. A simple question like "How many days does it take for a bean to sprout?" could be explored doing some Internet research as a class and also by conducting an experiment. These are simple distinctions teachers at any grade level could use to help students begin to understand the way in which scientific knowledge is formed.

SCIENTIFIC KNOWLEDGE IS OPEN TO
REVISION IN LIGHT OF NEW EVIDENCE

One of the most engaging things about science is that as a discipline, it is constantly changing. The old adage "when you know better, do better" helps us to better understand the way in which science changes in time. When scientists have access to better tools or more information, they are able to revise initial ideas in light of new evidence. For example, for a long time, the theory of continental drift developed by Alfred Wegener, a German geophysicist, was used to explain how Earth's plates moved over time, based on similar coastlines and living things on various continents. The idea of "Pangea" or a supercontinent (comprising all other continents) slowly separating and moving over time was the accepted scientific knowledge from the early 1900s until the 1950s. Later, scientists learned more about the structure of Earth's layers through the discovery of seafloor spreading, and the concept of plate tectonics replaced continental drift.

The motion of Earth's continents is hardly the only example of cases in which scientists learned more and revised their initial ideas. The magazine *Popular Mechanics* devotes an entire segment to ways in which scientific knowledge has changed over time in its "We've Been Wrong Before" column.[1] These are great examples to share with students to help them understand the ways in which science has changed and grown over time.

SCIENTIFIC MODELS, LAWS, MECHANISMS,
AND THEORIES EXPLAIN NATURAL PHENOMENA

One challenge to learning and thinking about science is that sometimes the terminology associated with science holds a similar but not the same

---

1. https://www.popularmechanics.com/weve-been-wrong-before.

meaning in everyday life. The best example of this challenge is with the word "theory." A quick dictionary.com search reveals there are as many as seven commonly known definitions of this term. The first is most closely aligned to the way in which we define a scientific theory and references Einstein's work on relativity: *a coherent group of tested general propositions, commonly regarded as correct, that can be used as principles of explanation and prediction for a class of phenomena.* Yet, within that same entry, the sixth definition describes the term quite differently: *contemplation or speculation.* With this much difference in two definitions of the same term from the same source, it's no wonder many find the idea of scientific theory confusing.

Yet other definitions provided on this common resource suggest that theories include some level of uncertainty. Ghose (2013) writes that a scientific theory "is an explanation of some aspect of the natural world that has been substantiated through repeated experiments or testing." This is the way in which the term is and should be used in reference to science.

Like theories, scientific laws are also based on a wide range of evidence to support claims. Yet, unlike theories, they do not provide a mechanism or explanation for natural phenomena. Figure 4.1 depicts the way in which we can distinguish between scientific theory and law.

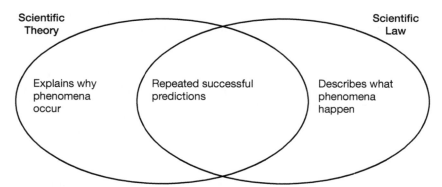

Figure 4.1 Scientific Theories and Laws.

Though both theories and laws can be amended as more information comes to light, they are both considered to be the best way we can explain natural phenomena. Theories and laws often rely on scientific models, or visual, mathematical, or verbal representations of ideas and systems.

SCIENCE IS A WAY OF KNOWING

As discussed earlier in this chapter, science is an epistemology or way of knowing the world. It is certainly not the only way of knowing, and individuals can often hold different or even conflicting views of how something works within their own understanding. And unlike some other ways of knowing or explaining the world, science can be used by others to think about phenomena in a systematic way. In a 2014 editorial, Lederman provides an example of having students pick the bones out of owl pellets to construct a skeleton of what the owl might have eaten. The author suggests, "Students can discuss how they made inferences about how the bones dissected fit together and how the form of each bone was used to infer something about its function and location in the skeletal system" (p. 9). This kind of discussion post-investigation allows the students to use scientific thinking and better understand how science can help them to know the world.

SCIENTIFIC KNOWLEDGE ASSUMES AN ORDER AND CONSISTENCY IN NATURAL SYSTEMS

One of the ways in which scientists are able to make predictions and inferences about phenomena is because of the system in which the universe acts. There are predictable patterns observable to even the youngest students that help explain the universe. Pointing out patterns of daylight, seasons, and simple life cycles such as butterflies or plants can help students understand the cyclic nature of the world around them. Knowing these patterns makes it easier to connect to more abstract ideas such as cell cycles or radioactive decay. One way to spot examples of pseudoscience is to identify ways in which patterns do or do not fit. For example, those who reject the idea that the Earth is round (such as the Flat Earth Society) cannot explain why the amount of light we receive at any given point on the planet is predictable and consistent day after day. A round and rotating Earth that revolves around the Sun can easily explain differences in daylight and darkness.

Another strategy for pointing out order in the universe is helping students look for hidden patterns in nature. The Fibonacci sequence or the Golden Ratio (1, 1, 2, 3, 5, 8, 13, and so on) can be observed in citrus fruit segments, seashells, sunflower seeds, and pinecones, but on the surface it might not be so noticeable to the casual observer. Asking students to consider everyday objects more closely, such as with the guidance of the diagram in figure 4.2, can make the organized and patterned nature of our universe clear. In the top half of this diagram, the box is divided into pieces relative to the Fibonacci sequence. In the bottom right corner, one box is divided into many. The smallest of the pieces is two triangles (representing 1, 1). Just above those triangles is a small square equal to the area of the triangles combined (representing 2). Just above that is a larger triangle with an area equal to the square and one triangle added together. The remainder of the top diagram demonstrates how the area increases according to the pattern in the Fibonacci sequence. The photograph of a snail demonstrates that the snail's shell grows according to this pattern as well.

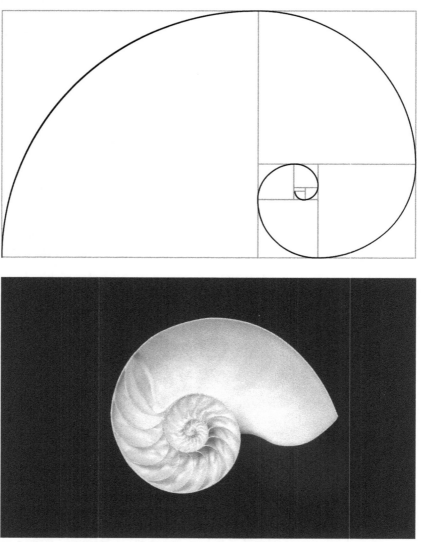

Figure 4.2 The Fibonacci Sequence in diagram and nature. (Top: Peter Dazeley, Getty Images; bottom: Kolonko, Getty Images)

SCIENCE IS A HUMAN ENDEAVOR

Like all people, scientists are human. This means that the act of engaging in science involves all the other shortcomings, limits, and bias involved with human thinking. Science, done by humans, exists within a culture and therefore exists within the limits of that culture. People without access to high-powered microscopes could not make the same kinds of observations as people with access to these complex tools. Similarly, different scientific disciplines make different assumptions and ask different kinds of questions. A biologist might be interested in the types of particles a cell's membrane lets in and out, while a physicist looking at the very same membrane might be more concerned with the speed of fluid movement across the membrane. Both scientists might understand or explain the structure and function of that same membrane in very different ways. The human part of science also allows for the possibility of changing ideas with more information as it becomes available.

It is also important to understand that scientific ideas have been discovered by more than one person—but the person whose story is told is often the person most like those doing the telling, and throughout history those people have most often been white and male. Recent research indicates that Babylonians calculated the distance between planets some two thousand years before Europeans were credited with doing the same. Other astronomical discoveries are well documented in Mayan, Chinese, and Indian history, yet these are not the accounts of discoveries we often read about in textbooks. For example, Halley's comet is known as the only short-period comet observable from Earth, normally more than once in a person's lifetime. It was last visible in 1986 and will be visible again in 2061. The comet was named for astronomer Edmond Halley in the early 1700s who documented its orbit. Yet records show that Chinese astronomers have tracked its orbit since about 250 BC.

This isn't to say that one should discount white male scientists at all. Rather, this is a reminder to be mindful of whose scientific accounts are shared and how.

SCIENCE ADDRESSES QUESTIONS ABOUT THE NATURAL AND MATERIAL WORLD

This final idea about NOS helps us to understand that there are limits to science. As discussed earlier, science itself is limited by cultural and technological constraints. Yet science is limited in the types of questions it can address. Scientific knowledge is based on empirical evidence and as such cannot cross boundaries to make judgments about moral, ethical, or aesthetic decisions. Medical science can determine the efficacy of chemotherapy but cannot make the decision whether the treatment or lack thereof will be more stressful for a family. Science cannot tell which kind of flower is the most beautiful or which dog breed is friendliest. The Understanding Evolution group (n.d.) goes on to give some more examples of where science is limited. Science is not democratic and therefore cannot be subject to popular opinion. Finally, science is nondogmatic. There is no belief in science—it is or it isn't.

TEACHING SCIENCE AT THE ELEMENTARY LEVEL

Elementary school teachers need not be experts in science and certainly not in all scientific disciplines. However, teachers do need to guide students to be good consumers of information and to be able to spot what is and isn't science. Familiarizing students with the characteristics of science can help prepare them to become informed citizens and decision makers.

AN EXAMPLE

Sometimes when explaining a phenomenon, one can get caught up in the process and explain it to children as "magic." But when we consider what science is and isn't, it's clear that thinking about the supernatural and ignoring evidence, reasoning, models, and patterns can confuse students. Consider showing the "hippy milk" demonstration. Add whole milk to a tray and make colorful dots using food coloring. Touch a wet cotton swab to the center of the tray. What happens? Next, put dishwashing liquid on the cotton swab and touch it to the center. What do you notice?

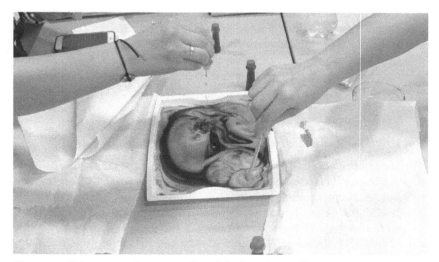

Figure 4.3 Images after soap is added to the milk and food coloring. (Lauren Madden)

Ask your students: How were the two trials different? What differences did you notice? Why do you think this happened? Was it magic or science?

Finally, you can explain that milk is made up of many different components including water, fat, sugars, and protein. The food dye stays in the water part. When you add detergent, the fat and protein parts become attracted to the food dye. This causes the milk to move as the different parts are rearranged, and the leftover food coloring makes interesting patterns. This activity can help teachers introduce students to the structure and function of components of milk, relating to the crosscutting concept within the NGSS that helps us explain that structure influences function throughout our universe.

CONCLUSION

This chapter provides guidance on what science is and how it works. Teachers and students alike can benefit from understanding what it means to know the world from a scientific perspective and to use science to explore questions and build explanations.

5

The Next Generation Science Standards

An Introduction

■ ■ ■

T he meme in figure 5.1 is funny but also represents what often comes to mind for teachers when they think about standards-based instruction in general. Standards can seem rigid and limiting for instructors, and teachers can become fearful that they'll lose creativity and intellectual freedom in classrooms that rely on standards-based instruction. Yet before condemning the idea of instructional standards, we should understand more about what standards are and how to use them to inform our teaching.

In this chapter, we will unpack some key ideas related to standards-based instruction in science. We will cover some historical perspective on how science standards emerged and have changed in the United States. We will also unpack each of the separate dimensions of the Next Generation Science Standards (NGSS), which are the most up-to-date science standards used in the United States.

Figure 5.1 Popular meme about standards in education. (Alexandra Hampton)

STANDARDS ARE NOT CURRICULUM

Several years ago, Karen Lamoreaux, a mother in Arkansas, created a video of herself criticizing the Common Core State Standards in Mathematics (CCSS-M) to her local school board, titled "Arkansas Mom Obliterates Common Core." The video went viral and inspired much news coverage and attention by the media (e.g., this article[1]). However, there was one small problem with her argument—it wasn't about the Common Core State Standards at all. It was about a poorly written set of problems in a textbook that had a sticker on it indicating the book was "aligned" to the Common Core. This can be confusing to parents, teachers, and students alike: if the book says it's aligned to the Common Core, isn't it?

_____

1. https://www.dailysignal.com/2014/01/17/arkansas-mom-poses-problem-common -core/.

The short answer is no. The Common Core is simply a set of topics and practices that students are expected to learn and use and can be found online at corestandards.org/Math. There are no prescribed teaching methods, problems, assessments, or activities for teachers. However, sometimes, when textbook companies publish their curricula, they state that these materials were written in alignment with the CCSS. And these materials sometimes *do* include prescribed teaching methods, problems, assessments, and activities. As a result, standards themselves and curricula written with those standards in mind can be conflated with one another and lead to confusion. It is critical that teachers know the difference between standards and curricula.

SCIENCE STANDARDS IN THE UNITED STATES

The NGSS were launched in 2013, several years after the widespread adoption of the CCSS in both mathematics and English language arts. They were written in alignment to the CCSS in both mathematics and English language arts. But their development was part of a much larger series of events related to science instruction over the past century and a half.

The idea of creating standards to dictate what science topics are taught and when is not new. In the 1890s, there was a boom in enrollment in secondary schools across the US, yet there were no standard curricula or even topics used in secondary schools. As a result, representatives from many universities and secondary schools were called together by the National Education Association to develop a curriculum to prepare students for higher education. The representatives, called the Committee of Ten, agreed that approximately 25 percent of the curriculum in secondary school should be devoted to the sciences including natural history (life and Earth science), physics, chemistry, and geology and gave advice on which specific topics within these content areas should be covered (DeBoer, 2019).

Later, during and after World War II, the numbers of scientists in higher education shifted significantly as scientists left universities for government positions. Then GIs returned home, many of whom went on to pursue college degrees on the GI bill. The need for scientists and engineers increased considerably, and this led to increased focus on science teaching and learning at the K–12 level. As the Cold War began, the National Science Foundation began to support many different research efforts to improve science teaching across the K–12 spectrum to prepare future scientists and engineers. This increase in attention led to the creation of many inquiry-based science curricula, many of which are still used in one form or another in classrooms today, such as Full Option Science Systems (FOSS) kits (DeBoer, 2019).

In 1985, the American Association for the Advancement of Science (AAAS) launched Project 2061. With Halley's comet visible, the scientists and educators at AAAS wondered about what changes in science and technology might take place by the next time the comet could be seen again—in the year 2061 (AAAS, 2013). Their work attempted to define what was meant by the term *scientific literacy* and yielded multiple publications. One, *Science for All Americans*, is a guideline for teaching and learning that "articulates and connects fundamental ideas in science without technical vocabulary and dense detail" (AAAS, 2013). They also created more detailed documents that delineate specific ideas in science, the *Benchmarks for Science Literacy* and the *Atlas of Science Literacy*. These documents offer an overarching perspective on the connections among and between science topics and ideas to be covered throughout elementary and secondary schools.

In 1996, the National Science Education Standards (NSES) were created by the National Research Council (NRC) to help shift science teaching and learning for K–12 away from memorization and rote tasks and toward inquiry-based explorations (NRC, 1996). This work was grounded firmly in the AAAS documents and focused on learning science for the purpose of understanding the world around us. These standards served as a baseline for individual states' standards and were written for bands of grade levels (K–4, 5–8, 9–12) to allow for individualization by states and school districts. The content standards were grouped into eight categories: (1) unifying concepts and processes in science, (2) science as inquiry, (3) physical science, (4) life science, (5) Earth and space science, (6) science and technology, (7) science in personal and social perspectives, and (8) history and nature of science. For nearly two decades, the NSES were the universal guidelines for teaching science.

THE NEXT GENERATION SCIENCE STANDARDS (NGSS)

In 2012, educators and scientists moved away from the vision for science teaching and learning outlined in the NSES and toward goals based on international benchmarking to help create future-ready students. The National Research Council released *A Framework for K–12 Science Education*. This framework included several key shifts from earlier standards, namely the NSES and the state standards that were written based on them. The three major shifts are: (1) no longer teaching science practices or the process of inquiry separate from science content; (2) introducing engineering content as early as kindergarten; and (3) providing grade level–specific standards rather than ideas for a range of grades such as K–4 or 5–8. The *Framework* became the document that guided the development of the NGSS. To date, twenty states have adopted the NGSS as their state standards. An additional twenty-four states have adopted ideas from within the *Framework* to craft their own state standards (described as "adapting" the standards rather than "adopting" them). Additionally the National Science Teaching Association aligns all of its materials and publications to the NGSS (NSTA, 2014).

So what does it mean to teach practices and processes of science along with content? The *Framework* introduced a *three-dimensional model* for learning. The three dimensions are: Disciplinary Core Ideas (DCI), Crosscutting Concepts, and Science and Engineering Practices. The three dimensions are combined in each *performance expectation* in the standards. Using all three dimensions together, teachers can focus on phenomena entirely rather than simply describing discrete scientific ideas separate from one another. We will get into each of the three in detail below, but it is helpful to think of this model with a cake analogy pictured in figure 5.2.

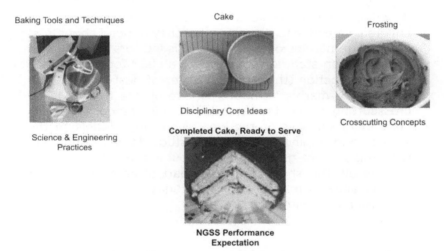

Baking Tools and Techniques

Cake

Frosting

Disciplinary Core Ideas

Crosscutting Concepts

Science & Engineering Practices

Completed Cake, Ready to Serve

NGSS Performance Expectation

Figure 5.2 Cake analogy for the NGSS. (Lauren Madden)

The performance expectation, or standard, is the final cake, ready to serve and eat. The cake itself represents the DCIs or the science content. The tools and techniques used to create the cake represent the science and engineering practices—in order to know the science, you must *do* the science. Finally, the crosscutting concepts are the frosting. These are the things that connect across scientific disciplines such as form and function and serve as the "glue" that holds scientific enterprise together. Together,

On a recent visit to elementary STEM specialist Mrs. Corevelyn's class, second graders were challenged to design "hand
pollinators" or tools for helping pass pollen from one flower
to another. The lesson was aligned to the following NGSS
Standard:

> 2-LS2-2. Develop a simple model that mimics the function
> of an animal in dispersing seeds or pollinating plants.

The second graders were working together and sharing out
initial ideas about what kinds of materials could best be used
to collect pollen from one flower and move that pollen to
a second flower. Some children suggested cotton balls and
were able to describe the way these fluffy objects could
carry the tiny grains of pollen in their fluff. Another group
suggested marbles. Mrs. Corevelyn pushed those children to
describe why they would choose such a smooth object. The
children were able to describe what they noticed about dust
sticking to marbles on a dry day. This led to a whole group
discussion on static electricity with a clear focus on structure and function (those tiny particles of dust were able to
stick to the marbles' smooth surface on the dry day), the
crosscutting concept that underlies this standard. Though
her initial focus was on the idea of building models, or the
science and engineering practice students were engaging
with, this student-generated share-out led to a shift in focus.
As a result, this short glimpse at part of an NGSS-aligned
activity allowed for a great opportunity to observe three-
dimensional learning in action.

the performance expectations help frame instruction of content in a way
that involves engaging in the scientific process and connecting to the
larger frame of scientific enterprise.

Disciplinary Core Ideas

"Disciplinary Core Ideas (DCIs) are the key ideas in science that have
broad importance within or across multiple science or engineering disciplines" (NRC, 2013e). The DCIs are grouped into four large categories:
Physical Science (PS), Life Science (LS), Earth and Space Science (ESS),

and Engineering (ETS). The topics that fall underneath each category are what one normally thinks of when considering what science *is* such as Chemical Reactions (PS1B), Wave Properties (PS4A), Natural Selection (LS4B), and Weather and Climate (ESS2D). Each performance expectation includes one DCI, and each idea develops across the K–12 spectrum using a model of learning progressions (i.e., one idea builds off another as children get older). Of the three dimensions of the NGSS, the DCIs are the most straightforward as they are what normally comes to mind when one thinks of science.

Crosscutting Concepts

The crosscutting concepts are the overarching ideas that connect across science disciplines, and help students to contextualize their understanding of content, or disciplinary core ideas: "When students encounter new phenomena, whether in a science lab, field trip, or on their own, they need mental tools to help engage in and come to understand the phenomena from a scientific point of view. Familiarity with crosscutting concepts can provide that perspective" (NRC, 2013c, p. 2).

One clear-cut example is cause and effect. In almost every science or engineering context, understanding cause-and-effect relationships is central to developing understanding. In the life sciences, we might ask a question about what happens when we have two plants and water one but not the other. In physics, we could explore how changing the surface of a ramp might influence the speed of a toy car. In both cases, young children can carefully consider the *cause* and *effect* of changing these conditions.

The NGSS include a total of seven crosscutting concepts. These are:

1. patterns;
2. cause and effect;
3. scale, proportion, and quantity;
4. systems and system models;
5. energy and matter: flows, cycles, and conservation;
6. structure and function; and
7. stability and change.

Appendix G of the NGSS (NRC, 2013c) details each of these concepts and provides specific examples of how each crosscutting concept develops across the K–12 spectrum. This appendix also provides reasoning for focusing our attention on the crosscutting concepts. This reasoning includes the importance of repetition of these ideas over time, identifying ideas that connect across scientific disciplines, and building a scientific vocabulary, among others. Children who are able to identify and interact with crosscutting concepts begin to develop scientific habits of mind, or ways of thinking about the world scientifically.

Science and Engineering Practices

The NGSS recognize that in order to learn and understand science, one must engage with *doing* science. Appendix F of the NGSS quotes the justification from the *Framework* as it outlines the importance of including practices in the NGSS:

> Standards and performance expectations that are aligned to the framework must take into account that students cannot fully understand scientific and engineering ideas without engaging in the practices of inquiry and the discourses by which such ideas are developed and refined. At the same time, they cannot learn or show competence in practices except in the context of specific content. (NRC, 2012, p. 218)

The importance of engaging in practices rather than simply using skills is central to the vision of the NGSS: practices require an understanding for *why* scientists and engineers do what they do (NRC, 2013b). For example, it is critical to purposefully plan scientific investigations, even with the youngest learners (with help from their teachers, of course). The skill of following a procedure absent of considering the planning and selection of appropriate methods does not mirror the work of scientists and constitutes "activity for activity's sake" rather than authentic science. The NGSS include eight specific science and engineering practices. These are:

1. asking questions (for science) and defining problems (for engineering);
2. developing and using models;
3. planning and carrying out investigations;
4. analyzing and interpreting data;
5. using mathematics and computational thinking;
6. constructing explanations (for science) and designing solutions (for engineering);
7. engaging in argument from evidence; and
8. obtaining, evaluating, and communicating information.

It should be clear that these practices are not often done in isolation; scientists often use them together in their investigations, and students in science lessons should as well. For example, using mathematical thinking and analyzing data almost always go hand-in-hand in science. Like the crosscutting concepts, the science and engineering practices develop in complexity over time. Appendix F of the NGSS includes a rationale for using these practices (NRC, 2013b). This appendix also provides a thorough justification for inclusion of each of these practices.

One key design element of the NGSS is that the science and engineering practices have direct connections to the practices of the Common Core State Standards in both English language arts (ELA) and mathematics (NRC, 2013a). These practices afford teachers an opportunity to point out skills that are critical in multiple disciplines. For example, constructing explanations is an essential skill in both ELA and science. Likewise creating and using models are common practices in mathematics and science. At the conclusion of appendix D of the NGSS, the diagram in figure 5.3 is provided.

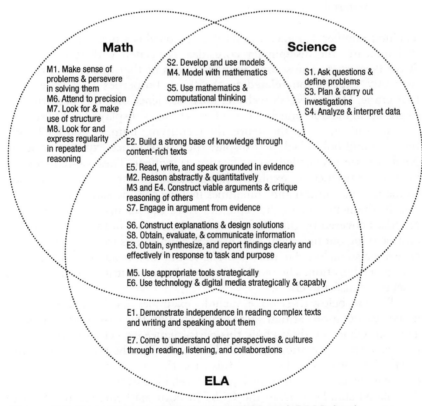

Figure 5.3 Common practices in the NGSS and CCSS, both mathematics and ELA. (Modeled on NGSS Appendix D.)

Thinking carefully about the way in which these practices allow students to engage in scientific enterprise *and* connect to other content areas can help teachers provide authentic and meaningful science learning experiences for their students.

Reading the NGSS

The three dimensions of the NGSS can certainly seem daunting and like a tremendous amount of information for a teacher to include in plans, and the standards themselves can be challenging to read. However, with some explanation, they can provide important information to teachers. Consider the following performance expectation (or standard):

> 1-PS4-1: Plan and conduct investigations to provide evidence that vibrating materials can make sound and that sound can make materials vibrate.

The first number, 1, indicates that this standard is a first grade standard. PS4 indicates the disciplinary core idea associated with this standard, Wave Properties. The second number 1 tells us that this is the first performance expectation related to the Wave Properties DCI covered in first grade. On the NGSS website, nextgenscience.org, this performance expectation includes much more information, as displayed in figure 5.4.

As you can see in the figure, the identifying number and DCI combination and bold black text display the performance expectation itself. Next, we see text called a clarification statement. These statements are helpful for teachers to explain what is meant by some terms in the performance expectation and sometimes include specific examples. The first box in the next row of the table describes the science and engineering practices covered by this performance expectation, in this case planning and carrying out investigations. Explicit connections to the nature of science are also included in this box. The second box restates the DCI along with an elaboration. The third box states the crosscutting concept; in this case, it is cause and effect.

The row below these boxes includes examples of other related performance expectations at that same grade level. In this case, there are none. The following row shows how this performance expectation connects to performance expectations covered before or after the target grade—this is called vertical articulation. In this case, the idea connects to a performance expectation at the fourth grade level. Finally, the last row provides the related standards from the CCSS in both mathematics and ELA to provide opportunities for interdisciplinary connections.

1-PS4-1 Waves and Their Applications in Technologies for Information Transfer

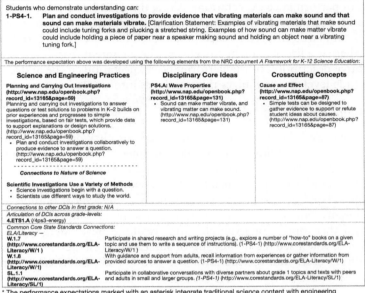

Figure 5.4 Sample NGSS performance expectation table. (NRC (2013c). Next Generation Science Standards: for states by states. National Academies Press)

Yes, this can seem like an overwhelming amount of information, but understanding how to read these standards can be tremendously helpful for planning effective lessons.

Using the NGSS

In order to locate the appropriate standards, you must visit nextgen-science.org. From there, it is possible to search for standards by grade level, DCI, crosscutting concept, science and engineering practices, or even keywords. The NGSS also offer tools for helping teachers to decide which standards to group together when planning year-long curricula or instructional units. For example, under the "Instruction and Assessment" drop-down menu on the NGSS home page, a link to existing units is provided by grade level. These can be used as-is or as a model for creating future units. Additionally under the "The Standards" drop-down menu, the option to "Read the Standards" pulls up another searchable arrangement of performance expectations. Along the right-hand side is a series of boxes. If you click the first box, "Standards by DCI," you can see a short list of standards covered at each grade level. However, on the right-hand side, there is a list of content storylines. These content storylines include a narrative description of the performance expectations to be addressed at the grade level and organizes the standards into similar topics.

A Challenge

Select one grade level (go to nextgenscience.org, click on "Instruction and Assessment," scroll down to "NGSS Storylines," and pick a grade band). Next read the content storyline for one grade in that band and observe how the standards are grouped together. Next pick one set of related topics and related performance expectations. Create a short outline of how you might address all three NGSS dimensions in a three-week science unit on this topic. For example, after reading the kindergarten NGSS storyline, you'll see the first group of standards presented is Motion and Stability: Forces and Interactions. The two NGSS performance expectations listed are:

> K-PS2-1. Plan and conduct an investigation to compare the effects of different strengths or different directions of pushes and pulls on the motion of an object.
> K-PS2-2. Analyze data to determine if a design solution works as intended to change the speed or direction of an object with a push or a pull.

Could you create a short outline of activities around this standard? Next select a different grade level and set of standards.

CONCLUSION

Standards are not curricula but rather guidelines that detail what content should be covered at a given grade level. Understanding the philosophy used to develop the NGSS can help situate teachers' planning. Knowing how to read the standards can be complex, but this is a necessary part of ensuring comprehensive science learning.

6

Asking Good Questions and Developing Lessons

■ ■ ■

Imagine a science lesson on sound. The teacher blows a whistle and asks the class, "Why did we hear the whistle?" The students, confused, might stumble on reasons such as "Because we have ears" or "Because you blew it." Though neither of those responses would technically be wrong, neither would address the content of how sound is created and travels. If instead, the teacher asked, "How is the sound different when we blow the whistle softly or loudly?" or "How is the sound different when you're close to the whistle or far away?" the students would be able to investigate the phenomenon of sound and learn more about how it works.

This chapter focuses on developing and using good questions in science. Questions are essential for sparking student interest and scaffolding instructional activities. We will cover several frameworks for categorizing and classifying questions. The second half of this chapter focuses closely on creating plans for lessons and units.

Sometimes the most challenging part of teaching is developing questions that engage our students. When teaching science, a discipline grounded in questions, as described more thoroughly in chapter 4, asking great questions becomes even more critical. In this chapter, we will offer several models for creating and using good questions, along with strategies for planning effective lessons.

PRODUCTIVE QUESTIONS

Elstgeest (2001) offers a model for questions that lead to scientific problem solving. She cautions readers to avoid questions that involve a lot of "wordiness" as those tend to be the sort of questions that have answers written in textbooks or class notes. This is similar to the *montillation of traxoline* example described in chapter 3 of this book. Elstgeest offers a model for **productive questions** or questions that stimulate critical thinking about science in children. The five categories of productive questions are: attention-focusing questions, measuring and counting questions, comparison questions, action questions, and problem-posing questions.

Attention-Focusing Questions

These are the simplest questions to ask and often result in focused observations and increased curiosity in children. For example, "What do you notice about the leaves of the plant?" directs students to focus on one part of a phenomenon and to observe it carefully from their own perspective. "Have you smelled anything different about the liquids?" can help students to use more than one sense to describe an observation and allow students to think carefully about similarities and differences.

Measuring and Counting Questions

These questions are also relatively straightforward. Measurement is a key part of the NGSS science and engineering practice *using mathematics and computational thinking*. Asking children, "How tall is that tower of bricks?" or "What is the volume of water in the graduated cylinder?" allows them to use mathematics to describe their observations.

Comparison Questions

This category of question helps students to think more critically about properties and observations. For example, "What is the same and different about these two powders?" engages students in classification and categorization based on similarities and differences. Noticing similarities and differences aligns with NGSS crosscutting concepts *patterns* and *stability and change*. These kinds of questions also allow children to pose further questions that could spark scientific exploration and investigation as well.

Action Questions

Action questions move past observation and inference and require some "doing" in order to answer. "What happens when you put a mealworm on a wet surface?" cannot be answered without actually moving the organism from one place to another, just as, "How does the speed of the car change when you put sandpaper on a ramp?" requires you to change a ramp's surface to answer a question. These are the sort of questions that teachers would generate in advance of a lesson and that serve as tools for structuring investigations.

Problem-Posing Questions

Much like action questions, problem-posing questions encourage students to explore and investigate. A teacher might ask: "Can you find a way to change the speed of a car on a ramp?" and this question would require students to generate their own strategies for experimentation. Thinking back to chapter 3 of this text, these kinds of questions demonstrate a more advanced level of inquiry during which children design their own tests and procedures.

BLOOM'S TAXONOMY

Perhaps the most well-known framework for classifying questions, *Bloom's Taxonomy* (see figure 6.1) offers teachers guidance on questions in terms of relative cognitive difficulty for students. Developed in 1956, this is a method for categorizing questions and can help a teacher to vary the intensity of the types of questions she asks. The categories are arranged in a triangle with those to be asked most frequently toward the bottom and those asked only occasionally toward the top.

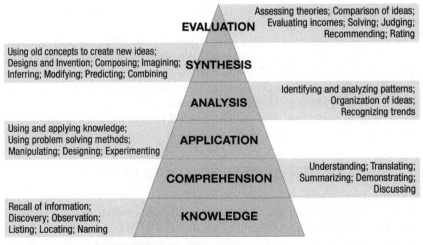

Figure 6.1 A model of Bloom's Taxonomy.

At the base of the questions is "Knowledge" or questions that involve recall and stating observations. Next on this scale comes "Comprehension," or the ability to summarize or explain information. The third level in Bloom's Taxonomy is "Application." Questions at this level require students to solve problems or use information in new contexts. The fourth level is "Analysis," which requires students to identify patterns and trends. The fifth level is "Synthesis," in which students use different types of information to form new ideas. The final or highest level of Bloom's Taxonomy is "Evaluation," which requires students to make judgments or establish solutions.

Several decades after its original introduction, an update was made to Bloom's Taxonomy: *Revised* Bloom's Taxonomy. In the revised version, each of the levels was renamed to a verb, and several were changed more significantly (e.g., "Knowledge" became "Remembering"). The framework retains the same purpose: to help teachers classify questions. Many tools exist to help teachers use these taxonomies effectively, such as the Edupress (2017) flip book of question starters to help teachers frame their own questions at a variety of levels of revised Bloom's Taxonomy and a multitude of tables and "verb" guides easily found on the Internet. The most important thing to consider when using Bloom's Taxonomy (the original or revised version) to write these questions is not the specific level of each individual question but rather thinking about questions *relative* to one another. For example, which of these questions would sit higher on the pyramid of Bloom's Taxonomy?

- Which moon phase comes after waxing crescent?
- How could you slow the process of water moving through a tube?

The second of these two questions requires a lot more critical thinking than the first and thus would be placed higher on Bloom's Taxonomy. The specific level is likely "Synthesis" as it requires you to use prior knowledge to address a new context. The first question on the other hand is at the "Knowledge" level as it requires just simple recall. However, these specific classifications are not needed to understand the usefulness of Bloom's Taxonomy as a tool.

OTHER MODELS FOR QUESTIONING

The productive questions and Bloom's Taxonomy frameworks are just a few ideas teachers can use to think critically about their use of questioning. Volger (2008) offers other models that can each be useful for different purposes and offers suggestions for ways to sequence questions. Some of those that are offered are starting with narrow questions and broadening out and the opposite (starting with broad and narrowing in). But some are a bit more detailed. For example, in the *extending and lifting* model Volger suggests, one might use questions that focus on certain elements of a specific topic and ask straightforward questions that require students to simply recall information. Later, this model expands to include questions that challenge students to make connections across ideas and apply information to new contexts. A third grade teacher might ask her students to describe the structure of a bird's beak by asking about many elements of the beak (e.g., How does it open? Is it pointed or round at the end? What does the inside of the beak look like?) before asking students how the beak allows that bird to survive well in a given habitat. Sequencing questions in this order helps to fully reach the three-dimensional goals of the associated NGSS performance expectation listed below.

> 3-LS4-3. Construct an argument with evidence that in a particular habitat some organisms can survive well, some survive less well, and some cannot survive at all.

Another strategy for structuring questions described by Volger is the *circular path* model in which the questions are sequenced in such a way that the teacher ends up right where she started. So a second grade teacher helping students to identify the types of evidence scientists use to determine whether something new is formed when mixing two substances together might ask a series of questions about whether a temperature, color, or phase change was observed and what that might tell us about the interaction between two substances being mixed.

Challenge: Consider the NGSS performance expectation below. Imagine you're a fourth grade teacher who took photos of the school playground weekly over the course of several months. In the photos, you can see puddles, ice, growing weeds, and dying grass. Draft a series of three questions you might ask during a lesson aligned with this standard:

> 4-ESS2-1. Make observations and/or measurements to provide evidence of the effects of weathering or the rate of erosion by water, ice, wind, or vegetation.

UNCOVERING STUDENT THINKING USING QUESTIONING

Everyone has misconceptions about *something*, but we generally don't know what ours are until we're confronted with an observation we can't explain. As we detailed in chapter 2, it is critical for teachers to build upon what children already experience about the world around them. However, as Abdi (2006) notes, "When correct, students' prior knowledge can be used as a building block for acquiring new knowledge. When incorrect, prior knowledge interferes with a student's ability to process new science concepts." Accessing prior knowledge and revealing student misconceptions can be a delicate balance for teachers. Students must feel comfortable enough to share their thinking whether or not it is scientifically accurate. Teachers must be able to aid students in confronting these ideas. One strategy teachers can use to prepare themselves is to become familiar with common scientific misconceptions. One great tool is the New York Science Teachers Association database.[1] Later on, in chapter 11 of this text, we will focus on formative assessment strategies that help us to reveal and address misconceptions through our instructional planning.

> Mr. Gomez told his fourth graders to make sure to wear warm clothes to school the next day, when temperatures were predicted to drop below freezing. Sarah, a student in his class, thought about this comment after school while she was making a snack and using the microwave to heat up a frozen pretzel. After she finished her snack, she took out a second frozen pretzel and put it inside one of her winter gloves and put it on the counter. She wondered if this piece of warm clothing might also heat up the pretzel.
>
> Later that evening, Sarah was surprised to find that the pretzel was still frozen in the glove and that the warm clothes didn't heat her snack. When she talked to Mr. Gomez about it the next day, he used it as an opportunity to talk about insulation and how warm clothes prevent loss of heat (or cold, in the case of the pretzel).

PLANNING INSTRUCTION

Planning effective questions can go hand-in-hand with planning effective science lessons. In order to establish a cohesive plan for teaching and learning, a teacher needs to identify *learning objectives* or specific and measurable goals. Objectives are straightforward and simple statements of what learners will be able to do by the end of the learning activities. Here are some examples:

---

1. https://newyorkscienceteacher.com/sci/pages/miscon/index.php.

- The second graders will be able to measure the height of the plant in centimeters.
- The learners will be able to identify three differences in properties of liquids and gases.
- The students will differentiate between sliding, hinge, and ball-and-socket joints.

A lesson might have one objective or several. These are the main "take-aways" from instruction and should help focus children on the most important ideas. By the end of a lesson, it should be clear whether or not the objective was met. Sometimes, teachers will share objectives with students early on in class. Other times, especially in the case of inquiry-based learning, the teacher might share the objective only after instruction has taken place to avoid cutting off the process of discovery for students. One important note of caution: avoid using words like *understand* or *familiarize* in your learning objectives. These terms are vague and difficult to measure.

Challenge: for each of the objectives above, identify a way that you could measure or assess whether they were met.

Backward Design

One popular model for designing lessons and instructional units is the backward design model. This model is part of a bigger educational philosophy: *Understanding by Design* (UBD) (Wiggins & McTighe, 2005). UBD-based instructional design makes use of Stephen Covey's *Seven Habits of Highly Effective People* to structure lessons and units (Covey, 2013). Though this text will not go into great depth on the UBD model, it will cover the basic principles of instructional planning, the "three stages model" of backward design (McTighe & Wiggins, 2012).

Stage 1 of this instructional model is to identify desired results. When considering NGSS-aligned teaching and learning, the first place to look is your selected standard. Let's return to the standard we considered earlier in this chapter:

4-ESS2-1. Make observations and/or measurements to provide evidence of the effects of weathering or the rate of erosion by water, ice, wind, or vegetation.

Some objectives that align to this standard could include:

- The students will describe observations of photographs taken of the same location once a month over the course of a year.

3 Stages of Backward Design

1. Identify Desired Results
What should students know, understand, and be able to do?

- Consider the goals, and examine standards and curriculum expectations.

- Specify important knowledge and skills.

- What are the big ideas and important understandings?

2. Determine Acceptable Evidence
How will we know if students have achieved the desired results?

- Think like an assessor before you think like a teacher.

- Determine the evidence that will prove understanding took place.

- Consider a range of assessment methods for contacting evidence.

3. Plan Learning Experiences & Instruction

What activities will provide students with the needed knowledge and skills?

- Design assessments prior to planning lessons.

- Determine the lessons and activities that need to be taught.

- Consider and plan activities that are effective for teaching the content.

Figure 6.2 Steps in the Backward-Design process based on McTighe & Wiggins (2012).

- The students will measure the depth of a stream outside the school monthly for one school year.
- The students will list changes in water and vegetation in a stream weekly for one month.

In Stage 2 of this process, the teacher will identify what evidence is needed to measure whether those objectives above were met. Some examples of evidence aligned with these standards are as follows:

- The students will describe observations of photographs taken of the same location once a month over the course of a year.
  The teacher will check for accurate descriptions in student notebook entries.

- The students will measure the depth of a stream outside the school monthly for one school year.
  The students will record data on a lab sheet that the teacher will compare to her own master sheet.

- The students will list changes in water and vegetation in a stream weekly for one month.
  The teacher will check for accurate descriptions in student notebook entries.

Once the teacher is able to clearly define objectives and assessments for learning, she can move on to planning instructional activities, or Stage 3 of the backward design process. Sometimes teachers use activities that are part of textbooks or science kits, while other times, teachers create or adapt materials specific to their own classroom and goals.

It should be emphasized that every district or school has its own preferred or sometimes required format for writing lesson plans. However, there are some common strategies all teachers can use to simplify the process.

1. **Identify standards, objectives, and assessments you intend to use.** This part, covered above, helps the teacher to focus the planning process.
2. **Consider your constraints.** Think carefully about materials available, time, classroom setup, available adult assistance, and number of students. These factors delineate exactly what is and is not possible to accomplish in a lesson.
3. **List the time frame of the lesson and materials you'll be using.**

4. **Select activities and create an outline.** If you're using activities you've found in a textbook or online resource, make sure to cite your references.
5. **Write questions with anticipated student answers.** Make sure to include some questions that help you to identify student misconceptions that might exist, and write questions at a variety of levels.

The process above is far from an exhaustive list for creating lessons but can be applied to nearly any teaching context to streamline the lesson-writing process. Take a moment to consider a science topic of interest to you. Using the list above, start strategizing what a lesson on that topic might look like.

On the pages that follow, you'll see one example lesson plan, written in a format particular to the college where I teach. It also uses the 5E Learning Cycle model (described in depth in chapter 3) to frame the inquiry-based learning experiences in this lesson. Use this as a guideline for thinking about lesson planning on your own on your topic of choice.

CONCLUSION

In order to effectively plan instruction, a teacher must have a plan in mind with specific objectives. All good lesson plans also include questions at a variety levels. Teachers should be able to anticipate possible answers to these questions and use those anticipated responses to help guide the sequence of activities.

CHAPTER 6 SUPPLEMENTARY LESSON: TERMITE TRAILS LESSON

Title: Termite Trails
This lesson is a modification of one created by Blake Newton, University of Kentucky.

Standards:
NGSS:

> 4-LS1-2. Use a model to describe that animals receive different types of information through their senses, process the information in their brain, and respond to the information in different ways.

Learning Objectives and Assessments:

Objectives	Assessments
The learners will be able to describe termite communication using pheromones.	W.I.L. entry in science notebooks describing learning outcomes (see attached sheet).
The learners will be able to design an investigation to test a claim about termite behavior.	Checklist (completed by teacher circulating the room) including: all students are participating in group investigation, materials and procedures are listed in science notebook entries, and data are being recorded in science notebooks.

Materials:
white paper
construction paper
assorted pens
markers
pencils
live termites
paintbrushes (for moving organisms)
handouts for science notebooks (see attached sheets)

Pre-lesson Assignments/Prior Knowledge:
Students will have already learned about some basic animal behaviors (e.g., eating, sleeping) and conducted several investigations in which they manipulated variables. Before this investigation, students will complete

safety and ethics contract, and the teacher will remind students about ethical and respectful treatment of live animals.

Lesson Beginning:
Engage
0:0:00–0:5:00

The teacher will ask students to list what they know about termites. Next, students will observe termites walking along a circle drawn with a pen on a sheet of white paper. Students will record observations and questions that arise in their science notebooks.

Instructional Plan:
Explore
0:5:00–0:20:00

- Teacher will ask students to develop a claim (or hypothesis) about the termite behavior.
- Each table group will decide on a procedure to investigate their claim.
- One student (the "getter") from each group will gather materials and bring them back to the table.
- Teacher will distribute five to ten termites to each table.
- Students will list materials and procedures in science notebooks.
- Students will conduct their initial investigation.
- Teacher will remind students that if they wish to modify their procedure and manipulate other variables, they may do so but must record these changes in their science notebooks.
- Teacher will remind students to record any data, evidence, or revisions to claims or predictions in science notebooks.
- Once students have finished exploring, students will record any initial findings or conclusions.

0:20:00–0:25:00

- Cleanup and materials return

Explain
0:25:00–0:30:00

- The teacher will facilitate a whole group discussion about the students' observations.
- The teacher will give a short lecture on termites and termite behavior, including communication using pheromones. Teacher

will also explain that a similar chemical to termite pheromones can be found in pen ink.
- The students will revise their initial conclusions based on the new information

Expand/Extend/Elaborate
0:30:00–0:35:00

- The teacher will provide examples of other animals that use pheromones to communicate.
- The teacher will pose the question: do you think humans use pheromones to communicate? The group will discuss the question and argue the possible answers.
- The teacher will share some evidence regarding human pheromones.

Evaluate
0:35:00–0:40:00

- Students will write a "What I learned" (W.I.L.) statement (or diagram) in their science notebooks.

Differentiation:

- Mixed-ability groups will be used so that more able learners can help less able learners.
- The teacher can provide sheets to use to help record and organize data in science notebooks for students who struggle with writing.
- Early finishers can manipulate additional variables and/or get a head start researching termites using texts and web-based resources.

Questions:

- Describe the termite behavior.
- Predict the outcome of your investigation.
- Do you think humans use pheromones to communicate?
- How does your evidence support or refute your claim?

Classroom Management:

- Students will complete a behavior and ethics contract prior to the investigation.
- Groups will meet at tables throughout the room so that the teacher has easy access to monitor behavior.
- Assigned students will collect materials and return them to the table.

Glue this sheet in your science notebook!
Termite Study

Part I:

Materials
3–5 live termites per group
ballpoint pens
white paper
paintbrushes

Procedure

- Draw several circles on white paper using ballpoint pen.
- Use paintbrushes to move termites onto paper.
- Observe termite behavior: record observations using words, diagrams, and/or pictures.
- Make a prediction about the termite behavior.
- With your team, design a procedure for testing your prediction (this is **Part II**).
- Test your prediction and record observations.
- Gather more information about termites (mini-lecture).
- Write a "What I Learned" (W.I.L.) conclusion statement.

Glue these sheets in your science notebook!
Termite Study

Part I Observations

Prediction
I think the termites _____

_____

because _____

_____.

Part II Procedure

_____

_____

_____

_____

_____

Part II Observations

Mini-lecture Notes

_____

_____

_____

_____

_____

W.I.L.

_____

_____

7

Connecting Science to Language Arts and Mathematics

■ ■ ■

When most people think back to their memories of elementary school, the image of a teacher sitting on a special chair and reading a compelling storybook to the class is often quick to come to mind. Reading is a critical part of the school day for all elementary-aged children. Another memorable part of elementary school might be memorizing multiplication tables or creating models of dodecahedrons. Like literacy, mathematics is central to the foundation of most elementary school teaching and learning. Unfortunately, memories of science learning don't always rise to the top for many students.

In this chapter, we will discuss purposeful strategies for connecting science to mathematics and English language arts in elementary school classrooms.

In the real world, science doesn't occur in a vacuum, and it shouldn't occur in isolation in the classroom either. Scientists use mathematics, reading, and writing in their work, and all problems must be considered with regard to social and cultural context. Research in neuroscience reveals a multitude of other benefits to integrated or multidisciplinary instruction. For example, considering an idea from the perspective of multiple disciplines can help facilitate multiple connections between existing pathways within the brain (Bernard, 2010). Further, interdisciplinary instruction helps students transfer prior knowledge to new concepts and identify relationships among ideas (You, 2017). STEM[1] and STEAM[2] are trends in education that focus on integrating instruction across multiple disciplines. We will discuss STEM and STEAM in detail in the next chapter of this textbook, but in this one, we'll focus on ways to integrate science with English language arts and mathematics.

Not surprisingly, most instructional time at the elementary school level is devoted to literacy and mathematics. Nationwide surveys of elementary school teachers indicate that mathematics and language arts are given more instructional time than other subject areas in the K–5 teaching and learning environment (Malzahn, 2013; NRC, 2013d; Trygstad, 2013). Malzahn (2013) and Trygstad (2013) reported on a large US study examining time devoted to each subject area in elementary teaching. The results indicated that elementary teachers reported they had much less time for science than math and language arts. For example, 99 percent of teachers reported that mathematics was done "all/most days." By comparison, only 24 percent of teachers reported that science was done "all/most days." This difference is reflected in the approximate minutes per day spent on subjects as well, where substantially more time was spent on language arts and mathematics than science: language arts (88), mathematics (55), science (20).

With such little time devoted to science on its own, teachers must find ways to integrate science content into other subject areas, and the most logical fit for this integration is language arts and mathematics, where the bulk of the instructional time is spent in elementary school settings. The diagram in figure 7.1 might look familiar from chapter 5 of this textbook: a figure from appendix D in the NGSS that identifies overlaps in practices among science, mathematics, and language arts.

Though this diagram focuses on the practice component of the NGSS standards, it provides a starting point for teachers considering ways to integrate across the content areas. For example, a persuasive writing assignment could easily be structured to integrate engaging in scientific argument from evidence when addressing the following third grade performance expectation:

> 3-LS2-1 Ecosystems: Interactions, Energy, and Dynamics. Construct an argument that some animals form groups that help members survive.

The possibilities of integrating writing into this standard are endless but could include watching live animal cams of various species in the

---

1. Science, Technology, Engineering, and Mathematics.
2. Science, Technology, Engineering, Arts, and Mathematics.

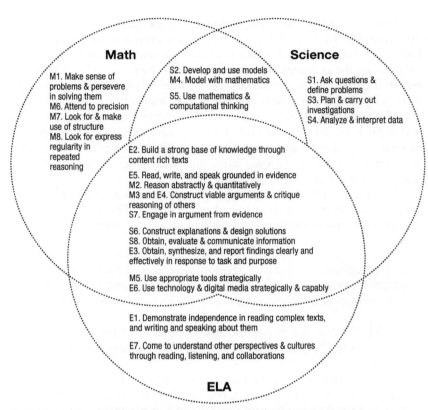

Math

M1. Make sense of problems & persevere in solving them
M6. Attend to precision
M7. Look for & make use of structure
M8. Look for express regularity in repeated reasoning

S2. Develop and use models
M4. Model with mathematics

S5. Use mathematics & computational thinking

Science

S1. Ask questions & define problems
S3. Plan & carry out investigations
S4. Analyze & interpret data

E2. Build a strong base of knowledge through content rich texts

E5. Read, write, and speak grounded in evidence
M2. Reason abstractly & quantitatively
M3 and E4. Construct viable arguments & critique reasoning of others
S7. Engage in argument from evidence

S6. Construct explanations & design solutions
S8. Obtain, evaluate & communicate information
E3. Obtain, synthesize, and report findings clearly and effectively in response to task and purpose

M5. Use appropriate tools strategically
E6. Use technology & digital media strategically & capably

E1. Demonstrate independence in reading complex texts, and writing and speaking about them

E7. Come to understand other perspectives & cultures through reading, listening, and collaborations

ELA

Figure 7.1 Common practices in the NGSS and CCSS, both mathematics and ELA.

wild alongside those from zoos and asking students to write a letter to the zoo making an argument whether more members of a given species should be living together. They could also observe any number of animals in a school yard or around a school building ranging from ants to deer over a given period of time and write about differences in group sizes for each type of animal.

Similarly, a mathematics lesson focused on using tools for measurement could explore mass and volume during instruction on the following fifth grade performance expectation:

5-ESS2-2 Earth's Systems. Describe and graph the amounts and percentages of water and freshwater in various reservoirs to provide evidence about the distribution of water on Earth.

One strategy for modeling this idea is to use paper clips. A standard box contains 1,000 paper clips, which can represent all the water on Earth. If 97.5 percent of water is in the oceans, then students can calculate how many paper clips represent that reservoir (975). Of the 25 remaining paper clips representing freshwater, 69 percent is frozen in glaciers (17 paper clips). Thirty percent is in groundwater (7.5 paper clips), and the remaining 0.5 percent or half a paper clip represents surface water. Fifth graders can be tasked with using fractions and percentages to create visual representations of these different water reservoirs, thus practicing their computational skills and visualizing the distribution of water on Earth's surface at the same time.

However, teachers can use more targeted teaching methods to integrate science into language arts and mathematics. The sections that follow provide some guidance and practical ideas for content integration.

In first grade, Ms. Smith's students explore differences in the amount of daylight we experience over the course of the school year, covering the following NGSS performance expectation.

> 1-ESS1-2. Make observations at different times of year to relate the amount of daylight to the time of year.

This year, she decided to introduce Greek mythology and the story of Artemis and Apollo, the children of Zeus and gods of sun and moon who fought terribly and constantly. They came to the compromise that one would rule for twelve hours of dark and the other for twelve of night, concluding the myth. After reading the myth aloud to her students, she presented the class's data on sunlight across the school year and asked whether the compromise was something we could observe. The children were then able to make connections between the myth and scientific data and have a rich discussion about stories and science.

ENGLISH LANGUAGE ARTS

Since the widespread adoption of the CCSS-LA, greater attention has been paid to the use of nonfiction and informational texts in the elementary years, and this poses some problems for teachers who may be more comfortable using familiar works of fiction. However, it also provides an opportunity for teachers to integrate science content into ELA instruction. This type of integration has been shown to enhance learning in both subjects.

"Students who have not been taught to set a purpose for reading and to use strategies to make sense of complicated informational texts may flounder when faced with the disciplinary learning demands in middle and high school. Preventing this decline requires a balanced approach to comprehensive literacy instruction, and balancing instruction means bringing science into the language arts classroom" (Madden et al., 2014).

In an earlier project (quoted above), I collaborated with a literacy educator and fourth grade teacher to create an integrated science and literacy instructional activity called *The Poetry of Dandelions* (Madden et al., 2014). The students analyzed a poem, "The Dandelion" (Withers, Brown, and Tate, 1920, p. 20), and informational text about controlling dandelions in lawns, "Controlling Dandelions in Lawns."[3] These two reading materials each focused on different structures of dandelions—their adaptations for seed dispersal and strong root structure. Next, the students observed dandelions and created labeled diagrams before discussing how plant structures influence their function. This lesson was not simply a science lesson or an ELA lesson but rather a truly integrated approach to explore both topics deeply. Table 7.1 details the various standards addressed by this lesson. The context of dandelions as a topic of debate, the strategies for removing them, and the structure and function of their bodies were considered together, allowing students to develop a nuanced and comprehensive understanding of the way these topics are interconnected.

Literature—ranging from children's books to technical reports—can provide detailed descriptions of living things and natural environments. In turn, the reader can reflect on and make sense of the pictures and words. *Crab Moon* (Horowitz, 2004) is a realistic fiction children's book that describes the phenomenon of horseshoe crabs spawning on the beach en masse in June. The interactions between the crabs and their environment, features of the crabs' bodies that allow them to survive, and the cyclical changes associated with the moon are all described. A read-aloud of this book, coupled with observations of horseshoe crab specimens, can situate a learner in the context of the organism. A lesson plan addressing this content follows this chapter.

Ippolito and colleagues (2018) offer other suggestions such as using professional documents like weather reports as mentor texts to aid students in recording their own observations and predictions and also to

---

3. www.americanlawnguide.com/lawn-weeds/54-cont.

Table 7.1

Next Generation Science Standards (NGSS)	Common Core State Standards (CCSS)
• 4-LS1-1 Construct an argument that plants and animals have internal and external structures that function to support survival, growth, behavior, and reproduction. • Practice 7. Constructing explanations. • Practice 8. Obtaining, evaluating, and communicating information. • Crosscutting Concept 4. Systems and system models. • Crosscutting Concept 6. Structure and function.	• CCSS.ELA-Literacy.RL4.5 Explain major differences between poems, drama, and prose, and refer to the structural elements of poems (e.g., verse, rhythm, meter) and drama (e.g., casts of characters, settings, descriptions, dialogue, stage directions) when writing or speaking about a text. • CCSS.ELA-Literacy.RI.4.9 Integrate information from two texts on the same topic in order to write or speak about the subject knowledgeably. • CCSS.ELA-Literacy.RI.4.4 Determine the meaning of general academic and domain-specific words or phrases in a text relevant to *grade 4 topic or subject area.* • CCSS.ELA-Literacy.RI.4.3 Explain events, procedures, ideas, or concepts in a historical, scientific, or technical text, including what happened and why, based on specific information in the text. • CCSS.ELA-Literacy.RI4.10 By the end of the year, read and comprehend informational texts, including history/social studies, science, and technical texts in the grades 4–5 text complexity band proficiently with scaffolding as needed at the high end of the range.

Note: Complete performance expectations, crosscutting concepts, and science practices are all listed for the NGSS.

get in the practice of using scientific language. These authors also suggest that examples of scientific writing can be used as a strategy for generating student questions and sparking the research process. These strategies are using reading and writing alongside scientific exploration—as sources of information that encourage further questioning, explanation, and sense-making on the part of the students. The reading and writing alone are not sufficient; rather they are complements and supplements to effective elementary science activities.

Language arts at the elementary level is not limited to reading and writing alone. Listening, watching, dramatic play, and artistic representation contribute to a nuanced and comprehensive language arts experience. Increasingly, podcasts are being used as tools for enhancing literacy instruction.[4] Godsey (2018) presents a suite of benefits of using podcasts in the classroom. One such benefit is that podcasts can help students develop confidence *decoding* texts through audio clues such as tone and cadence of speech when transcripts are used alongside audio recording. Another benefit is that podcasts expose readers and listeners to a variety of sources of narrative text. Finally, listening to podcasts can engage easily distracted students in a way that reading alone cannot. *Radiolab,* a podcast and radio program aimed at communicating scientific information, can be an excellent mechanism for exploring science and literacy together. One episode, "The Goo and You," requires listeners to think carefully about a common phenomenon addressed in the elementary years—the butterfly life cycle (WNYC, 2014). Though much is known and can be learned about the things we can observe about butterfly life cycles from egg through adult, this episode of *Radiolab* tells the story of what happens inside the chrysalis. This episode inspired writer and professor Tabitha Dell'Angelo to write a nonfiction children's book, *Butterflies: The Strange and Real Story of How a Caterpillar Turns into a Butterfly.* Together, these resources can inspire students to wonder and ask questions about the unknown while simultaneously exploring patterns and structures in the world around them.

The following NGSS performance expectation at the third grade level is well aligned with this integrated literacy and science activity.

3-LS1-1 Develop models to describe that organisms have unique and diverse life cycles but all have in common birth, growth, reproduction, and death.

The CCSS-LA standard below is also met through this activity.

CCSS.ELA-LITERACY.RL.3.1 Ask and answer questions to demonstrate understanding of a text, referring explicitly to the text as the basis for the answers.

---

4. For more strategies on integrating podcasts into your teaching, see chapter 9 of this text.

MATHEMATICS

Science and mathematics are often thought of together. It isn't uncommon to hear someone say that mathematics is the language of science. With recent attention focused on STEM, oftentimes it is simply assumed that science and mathematics are already taught together.

Brown (2004) recalls a science teaching experience about landforms and notes that the mathematics is *implied* but not explicit. Unfortunately, this assumption that mathematics is part of all science instruction is often the case. Brown reflected on her teaching and noted that the mathematics she did incorporate—measuring heights and depths, computing volume, and describing shapes—occurred more due to happenstance than planning. She suggested that in the future mathematics lessons should be aligned to inquiry-based science explorations in order to ensure students have the appropriate problem-solving tools to fully engage with the science content. Though these recommendations are excellent, they fall short of offering guidance for teaching mathematics and science in an integrative approach.

As we mentioned earlier, there are many mathematical skills that overlap with the science practices, namely using mathematics and computational thinking, creating and using models, and modeling mathematically. Bossé and colleagues (2010) offer another perspective on the similarity of skills in the two subjects. They offer a framework that identifies overlaps in the 5E Learning Cycle (see chapter 3 of this text for more information on that cycle) and the National Council for Teachers of Mathematics (NCTM) principles and standards. This article expands the overlaps in the two subjects and includes a broader perspective simply identifying the common practices; for example, the idea of reasoning and proof as a topic that spanned both domains. Proof-writing in logic and geometry requires the student to consider evidence with respect to a claim (e.g., these two triangles are similar). The process of scientific explanation, or the third E in the 5E Learning Cycle, uses a very similar approach. Bossé and colleagues also identify communication of content as a key topic shared between the two content areas. When teachers can point out the ways in which their students' work is similar across content areas, they enhance salience and coherence for their students. Johnson (2011) discusses several studies that also showed that conceptual understanding in both mathematics and science was enhanced when the subjects were taught together. He offered some novel solutions to help teachers collaborate with one another such as using Google Hangouts or video calls to connect teachers during instruction.

Science lessons can provide context for mathematical phenomena for students. Consider the following NGSS performance expectation at the second grade level:

2-PS1-1. Plan and conduct an investigation to describe and classify different kinds of materials by their observable properties.

A teacher might tell students that some people prefer large ice cubes while others like crushed ice or the smaller pieces of ice that come with fountain drinks. The students could then describe the shape of the ice in a few different forms and test to see how their geometric shape influences how long they stay frozen and keep a glass of water cool. This investigation also directly engages students with the following NCSS-M standard in an authentic real-life context:

CCSS.MATH.CONTENT.2.G.A.1. Reason with shapes and their attributes.

This activity covers two important ideas: the properties of the material—frozen water—and describing the shape and size of the ice.

Games can also be a fun and interesting way to connect science and mathematics when considering authentic real-world problems. Consider this real-world problem: one way of meeting humans' energy demands is through using offshore wind farms or turbines as energy sources. But scientists and engineers must be careful when selecting where to place these farms as the turbines can harm migrating bird populations. They must consider both wind patterns and migration patterns when making decisions about location.

Remember the popular board game Battleship? As a refresher, in this game, players are paired and arrange a series of ships on a coordinate plane. One player calls out a location of that plane, and the other lets their partner know whether that location was a "hit" or "miss." In mathematics, coordinate planes are introduced in fifth grade. In science, fifth graders study interactions between the geosphere, hydrosphere, biosphere, and atmosphere. A Battleship–type model could help students explore both these important topics.

Teachers can easily download blank Battleship templates and draw in wind paths and bird migration paths in two different colors.[5] They can

---

5. You may wish to consult local maps or simply draw long straight or curved lines to demonstrate these different paths.

then pair students and ask them to "play" Battleship Windfarm. Instead of just two possible outcomes, hit or miss, there are four:

- Miss (M): location is not on the path of the wind.
- Hit (H): location is on the path of the migrating birds.
- No Build (N): location is on the path of the wind but also on the path of the migrating birds.
- Build (B): location is on the path of the wind and not on the path of the migrating birds.

Teachers can tell their students to write the corresponding letter on their Battleship grid and play any number of rounds of the game. The winner is the student who has the largest number of Bs on their grid in the end. A lesson plan that describes this activity in more detail is included following this chapter.

This game requires students to use the coordinate plane to find locations and to think about interactions between the atmosphere (wind) and biosphere (birds) to consider solutions for a real-world problem using the fun and familiar format of a Battleship game. The NGSS and CCSS-M standards addressed in the game are as follows:

CCSS.MATH.CONTENT.5.G.A.1. Graph points on the coordinate plane to solve real-world and mathematical problems.
5-ESS2-1. Develop a model using an example to describe ways the geosphere, biosphere, hydrosphere, and/or atmosphere interact.

USING THE STANDARDS TO
HELP BUILD INTEGRATED LESSONS

One key strength of the structure of the NGSS is that the connections to specific CCSS-LA and CCSS-M standards are explicitly provided for teachers. See figure 7.2 of an NGSS performance expectation about weather at the kindergarten level. In chapter 5 of this text, the general structure and format of the standards were detailed. The tables that display each performance expectation contain a tremendous amount of information that can certainly be overwhelming for any reader. A teacher with an eye toward integrating science into language arts and mathematics can focus on the very bottom row of this table for direct links to the related ideas in these other content areas. This information can certainly be used to help structure interdisciplinary lessons and units or even to help teachers sequence content in a way that is supportive of interdisciplinary instruction.

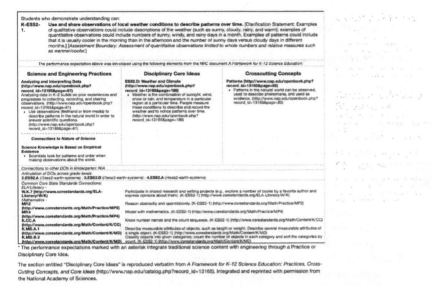

Figure 7.2 An example NGSS standard highlighting connections to ELA and mathematics. (NGSS Lead States [2013]. Next Generation Science Standards: for states by states. National Academies Press)

These suggested disciplinary connections are tremendously helpful, but teachers shouldn't feel limited by them either. In the earliest years, classroom instruction often crosses disciplinary borders. A kindergarten teacher addressing the standard above is sure to integrate a multitude of activities from having students verbally describe weather conditions to asking them to graph the number of rainy days in any given month. These kinds of natural connections that are commonplace in early childhood settings are often replaced with more intensive and discipline-specific instruction as children get older. Those tried-and-true strategies for obvious connections are some simple ways to ensure our students are connecting science to real-life experience and making sense of the world around them.

CHAPTER 7 SUPPLEMENTARY LESSON A:
HORSESHOE CRAB LESSON

Title: Literature-Centered Horseshoe Crab Observations

Topic: Habitats and organisms

Essential Question: How are living things different in different habitats?

Standards:
NGSS:

> 2-LS4-1. Make observations of plants and animals to compare the diversity of life in different habitats.

CCSS-LA:

> W.2.7 Participate in shared research and writing projects (e.g., read a number of books on a single topic to produce a report; record science observations). (2-LS4-1)
>
> W.2.8 Recall information from experiences or gather information from provided sources to answer a question. (2-LS4-1)

Learning Objectives and Assessments:

Objectives	Assessments
The learners will be able to record observations of horseshoe crabs.	Teacher will check science notebooks for written and drawn observations.
The learners will be able to describe the ways in which horseshoe crabs are suited for their marine environment.	Teacher will listen for description of the physical features of the horseshoe crab that allow it to live in water and lay eggs on the beach.
	Teacher will check students' "What I learned" statements in science notebooks for evidence of horseshoe crabs' suitability for their environment.

Materials:
photographs or specimens of horseshoe crabs
Horowitz, R. (2004). *Crab moon*. Somerville, MA: Candlewick Press.

Pre-lesson Assignments/Prior Knowledge:
Students may have visited the beach and may have observed horseshoe crabs in the past. Students will have conducted other observations of organisms and their habitats.

Lesson Beginning (5 minutes):
The teacher will ask students whether they have seen horseshoe crabs. Students will describe their experiences with these animals. All comments will be accepted.

Instructional Plan:
0:5:00–0:15:00

- The teacher will ask students to observe photographs and/or specimens of horseshoe crabs.
  - Teacher will remind students of safety concerns and safety contracts when observing specimens.
- The students will write and draw their observations in science notebooks.

0:15:00–25:00

- The teacher will read *Crab Moon* aloud to the class.
- She will pause periodically to draw students' attention to various features of the organisms highlighted in the book and ask clarifying questions throughout the reading.

0:25:00–35:00

- The teacher will ask the students a variety of questions:
  - Where do horseshoe crabs live? Do they ever live elsewhere?
  - How do horseshoe crabs' bodies help them to survive?
- The teacher will direct the students to write a "What I learned" statement in their science notebooks describing if and how the horseshoe crab is well suited for its environment.

Closure:
The lesson will conclude with students writing a "What I learned" statement in their science notebooks.

Differentiation:

- The teacher can provide sheets to use to help record and organize data in science notebooks for students who struggle with writing.
- Early finishers can submit an "I wonder" question to the teacher suggesting another possible experiment about changes.

Questions:

- Have you ever seen a horseshoe crab? Where?
- Describe the horseshoe crabs' bodies.
- Where do horseshoe crabs live? Do they ever live elsewhere?
- How do horseshoe crabs' bodies help them to survive?

Classroom Management:

- The teacher will circulate the room throughout the observation period to avoid disruptions.
- The students will review safety rules before handling specimens, and the teacher will draw attention to the science safety contract.

CHAPTER 7 SUPPLEMENTARY LESSON B:
BATTLESHIP WIND FARM

Demonstration Lesson Plan Integrating Science and Mathematics

Title: Battleship Wind Farm

Standards:
NGSS:

> 5-ESS2-1 Develop a model using an example to describe ways the geosphere, biosphere, hydrosphere, and/or atmosphere interact.

CCSS-M:

> CCSS.MATH.CONTENT.5.G.A.1 Graph points on the coordinate plane to solve real-world and mathematical problems.

Learning Objectives and Assessments:

Objectives	Assessments
The students will be able to identify interactions between the biosphere, atmosphere, and designed world.	Students will successfully use the provided coordinate plane to identify appropriate locations for wind farms.

Materials:
For each pair of students:
Battleship template with sample wind patterns (teacher will mark using blue curved lines) and bird migration patterns (teacher will mark using red curved lines). Use different patterns for each student in the pair.

Pre-lesson Assignments/Prior Knowledge:
Students will have already used coordinate planes to plot points on a graph. Students should know that winds follow predictable patterns and that many birds and other animals migrate.

Lesson Beginning (5 minutes):

- Ask students about wind energy. Show this short video[6] to demonstrate what offshore wind farms look like.
- Ask students to brainstorm what factors they might need to consider when deciding where to place a wind farm. Record ideas on the board.

Instructional Plan (20 minutes):

- Pair students and distribute grids.
- Review procedures for playing Battleship: Partner A calls out a location on their partner's graph. Partner B marks that coordinate with one of the following.

    - Miss: location is not in the path of the wind. Draw an M on the grid.
    - Hit: location is on the path of the bird migration and could harm birds. Draw an H on the grid.
    - No Build: location is on the path of the wind but also on the path of the bird migration. Draw an N on the grid.
    - Build: location is on the path of the wind and NOT in the path of bird migration. Draw a B on the grid.

- Ask them to play ten rounds of "Battleship" following the procedure above.
- The student with the most Bs or turbines wins the round. Repeat if time allows.

Closure:
As a whole class, discuss the pros and cons of building offshore wind turbines. Discuss how engineers use science and math in their work to build solutions to real-life problems.

Differentiation:

- Mixed-ability pairs will be used to ensure those who struggle with the content can assist one another.
- Teachers can provide a list of rules for students who need them.
- Early finishers can repeat the game until time runs out.

---

6. https://greencoast.org/onshore-vs-offshore-wind/.

Questions:

- Where did you get the most Bs or "builds"?
- What other kinds of factors do you think engineers need to know when planning wind farms?
- What do you think would happen if you chose to build outside of the wind path?

Classroom Management:

- Teacher will circulate the classroom to ensure students are on-task throughout the activity.

8

STEM and STEAM

Creativity and Problem-Solving in Elementary Science

■ ■ ■

If there were just one buzzword that could be used to mark the current state of education, it would be STEM, or Science, Technology, Engineering, and Mathematics. Across the country, schools are implementing STEM clubs, integrating design challenges into their classrooms, and starting robotics teams in an effort to incorporate STEM into the curriculum. Not far behind STEM is STEAM, or Science, Technology, Engineering, *Arts*, and Mathematics. STEAM emphasizes the creative side of integrated curriculum. Similarly, other acronyms related to STEM seem to pop up every day. e-STEM can refer to environmental STEM or electronic STEM, depending on the context. Likewise iSTEM can mean integrat*ed* or integrat*ive* STEM. Throughout this chapter, we will explore what is meant by STEM and STEAM and how we can use these approaches to foster creative thinking and problem-solving in elementary classrooms.

In this chapter, we will define and discuss STEM and STEAM along with ways to use them in science lessons. This chapter includes a sample lesson created by past science methods students integrating art into science instruction as an example STEAM lesson.

WHAT IS STEM ANYWAY?

Though STEM is near ubiquitous in schools, there is no one clear definition for what STEM is. It can refer to any one of the four STEM disciplines, so a biology teacher could easily call herself a STEM teacher. It can also refer to instruction that is interdisciplinary—combining one or more of the STEM disciplines together in a single lesson or unit. The acronym STEM was first coined by the National Science Foundation (NSF) more than two decades ago and has been in popular use since (Sanders, 2009). The end goal of STEM education is typically to engage students with problem-solving and critical thinking. For simplicity's sake, we will take an integrative approach to define STEM in this chapter. *Integrative STEM uses multiple STEM disciplines to make meaning and solve problems.* This means that when we refer to STEM instruction, we're talking about lessons that include more than just one STEM discipline (e.g., science PLUS engineering, technology, and/or mathematics).

The Engineering Design Process

One feature of STEM teaching and learning that often emerges is the **engineering design process.** Much like STEM as a discipline, there exist a multitude of models for this process, and these can range from a simple three-step format as referenced in the NGSS appendix I (NRC, 2013e) to one that contains ten or more steps. The model in figure 8.1, created by Karsnitz and colleagues (2012), is an iterative five-step process that teachers and students can use collaboratively to structure investigations. Typically, the cycle starts with **ask**, emphasizing the problem-solving component of STEM. In this phase, students and teachers pose a question or identify a problem to explore. Next comes **imagine.** During this phase, students envision possible solutions or outcomes. In general, this part of the process takes place in small groups or pairs, rather than with individuals or in whole class environments. However, every situation is different and sometimes allowing independent time for imagination can lead to more productive outcomes. The third step is to **plan** investigations. Students identify resources, materials, and a time frame. Teachers or curricular materials often set parameters for exploration during this phase with respect to materials and or time. The planning is followed by the **create** phase, during which students build prototypes or models to test. The time set aside for creating is often the biggest part of a design challenge, allowing students time to use materials and apply what they have learned. The final step is **improve**, during which students examine the results of their creative endeavors and modify them to generate better solutions. This step often occurs after students share out their products

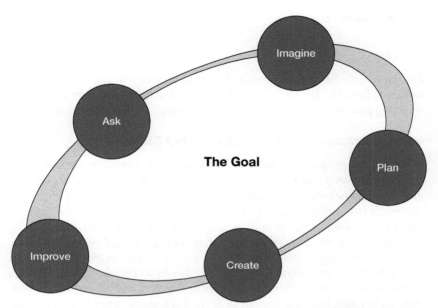

Figure 8.1 A 5-step model of the Engineering Design Process based on Karsnitz et al. (2012).

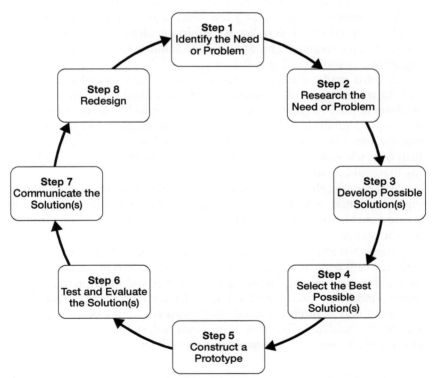

Figure 8.2 A more complicated 8-step model of the engineering design process based on the Massachusetts Department of Education's model.

and have time to compare and contrast their work to the work of classmates. Often, the students move back and forth between the create and improve phases many times in a STEM lesson to create ideal solutions.

Some Examples of STEM in Elementary Classrooms

In an earlier project (Madden & Turner, 2018), a teacher-partner and I used the five-step engineering design process to help first graders investigate reasons beavers build dams and create model dams using everyday materials (food products, clay, rocks, and sticks) mimicking the beavers' process. The similarities in engineered, or human-created, dams and those created by beavers themselves were that they were used to stop the flow of water and help catch fish. After creating model dams, the students tested their models using water and dry beans to represent fish. Though some dams let some water through, most did not, and all served the purpose of keeping fish in a specific area, making them easier to catch. Each group observed the others' models and then improved their initial plans based on what was successful for others.

Recently, I visited a third grade class at a school that created a pond in their outdoor learning area a few years ago. Last autumn, the pond was bombarded with falling leaves, requiring extensive, time-consuming, and expensive cleanup. This autumn, the buildup of leaves was already beginning, as shown in figure 8.4.

A third grade teacher and the school's STEM specialist partnered to help students generate solutions to the leaf-filled pond problem. The students needed to create some kind of barrier to block the leaves from entering the pond that also allowed frogs and salamanders to enter and exit the pond as needed. The students worked in small groups with the help of teachers to plan solutions and build prototypes using real building materials, as shown in figure 8.5.

After testing their models with real leaves and toy frogs and improving upon initial models, the STEM teacher worked with colleagues to create a usable structure that helps keep the pond in good shape throughout the winter.

These two examples of STEM in elementary classrooms demonstrate some of the integrative subject's best utility. In the first example, students were able to truly engage in testing the structure and function of designed objects and better understand animal behavior in a hands-on way. This is a topic that is often explored solely through books or video. In the second, the students were able to generate solutions to a problem that affected their own school, engaging in an authentic real-world context.

Figure 8.3 Prototypes of beaver dams. (Jill Turner)

Figure 8.4 A pond covered in leaves. (Lauren Madden)

Figure 8.5 Third graders designing models of covers for the pond.
(Lauren Madden)

STEM and Failure

In one of his most famous songs, "Love Minus Zero/No Limit," folk singer Bob Dylan said, "There's no success like failure, and failure's no success at all." One important part of STEM education is that it includes failure! In fact, failure is one of the most crucial parts of learning. Students who see their designs fail are able to identify strengths, shortcomings, and opportunities for growth. Identifying how, why, and where ideas or plans fail is a necessary part of developing solutions. Yet this can be a challenge for many teachers. Students, especially those raised in our testing-centric school culture, are sometimes reluctant to admit failure. Creating opportunities to celebrate failure through the use of the design process helps teachers to build resilience in their students. On a recent visit to a local school, I saw an "epic failures" classroom display. By making failed attempts central to class discussion and something teachers can help students to celebrate, teachers can ensure that their students are seeking opportunities for growth.

This kind of work is helpful to social-emotional learning as well. In many schools, teachers encourage students to adopt a *growth mindset* (Dweck, 2015). A growth mindset is one that re-examines students' failures. While a fixed mindset might result in a student saying, "I can't do it," a student with a growth mindset might say, "I can't do it *yet*." It requires students to become reflective doers of science and STEM and helps to focus effort on identifying areas for improvement and learning. Failures in STEM investigations are ideal opportunities to help foster growth mindset mentalities in students.

STEM also provides teachers with opportunities to engage students in *productive struggle*. Popularized by mathematics educators, productive struggle occurs when lessons are structured in a way that requires students to think about multiple solutions to a problem, evaluate evidence, and reflect in order to make sense of a concept. As Warshauer (2015) notes, "By incorporating instructional approaches that acknowledge student struggles and effectively support and guide the students' thinking toward a productive resolution, students are given opportunities to strengthen their disposition toward engaging in challenging tasks." By their nature, STEM activities are rich in opportunities for productive struggle and can lead to deeper and more comprehensive understandings of science content. One suggestion to incorporate productive struggle into science or STEM instruction is to praise students for considering multiple perspectives, acknowledge when they rule out insufficient explanations, and identify progress along the way. In this way, teachers can draw attention to the strengths of the process rather than the lack of successful solutions.

STEM AND THE NGSS

One way that the NGSS are quite different from prior science standards is their integration of engineering design standards. They include an entire domain of Disciplinary Core Ideas (DCIs) called "Engineering, Technology, and Applications of Science," abbreviated ETS. Performance expectations that include these DCIs are sometimes unlike those in other scientific domains in that they are not written for one specific grade level. Rather, they are written to address a span of grades: K–2, 3–5, middle school, and high school. This allows for an iterative approach to STEM education, allowing teachers across multiple grade levels to circle back to similar design challenges and build ideas upon one another. See the example K-2 DCI in figure 8.6.

Students exploring the performance expectation below could be testing what shape pot is best for growing a plant with shallow roots or which kind of clothing is best for riding down a slide on the playground.

K-2-ETS1-2 Engineering Design

Students who demonstrate understanding can:

K-2-ETS1-2. Develop a simple sketch, drawing, or physical model to illustrate how the shape of an object helps it function as needed to solve a given problem.

The performance expectation above was developed using the following elements from the NRC document *A Framework for K-12 Science Education*:

Science and Engineering Practices	Disciplinary Core Ideas	Crosscutting Concepts
Developing and Using Models (http://www.nap.edu/openbook.php?record_id=13165&page=56) Modeling in K-2 builds on prior experiences and progresses to include using and developing models (i.e., diagram, drawing, physical replica, diorama, dramatization, or storyboard) that represent concrete events or design solutions. (http://www.nap.edu/openbook.php?record_id=13165&page=56) • Develop a simple model based on evidence to represent a proposed object or tool. (http://www.nap.edu/openbook.php?record_id=13165&page=56)	**ETS1.B: Developing Possible Solutions** (http://www.nap.edu/openbook.php?record_id=13165&page=206) • Designs can be conveyed through sketches, drawings, or physical models. These representations are useful in communicating ideas for a problem's solutions to other people. (http://www.nap.edu/openbook.php?record_id=13165&page=206)	**Structure and Function** (http://www.nap.edu/openbook.php?record_id=13165&page=96) • The shape and stability of structures of natural and designed objects are related to their function(s). (http://www.nap.edu/openbook.php?record_id=13165&page=96)

Connections to K-2-ETS1.B: Developing Possible Solutions to Problems include:
Kindergarten: K-ESS3-3 (/kess3-earth-human-activity), **First Grade:** 1-PS4-4 (/1ps4-waves-applications-technologies-information-transfer), **Second Grade:** 2-LS2-2 (/2ls2-ecosystems-interactions-energy-dynamics)

Articulation of DCIs across grade-levels:
3-5.ETS1.A (/3-5ets1-engineering-design) ; **3-5.ETS1.B** (/3-5ets1-engineering-design) ; **3-5.ETS1.C** (/3-5ets1-engineering-design)

Common Core State Standards Connections:
ELA/Literacy –
SL.2.5 (http://www.corestandards.org/ELA-Literacy/SL/2) | Create audio recordings of stories or poems; add drawings or other visual displays to stories or recounts of experiences when appropriate to clarify ideas, thoughts, and feelings. *(K-2-ETS1-2)* (http://www.corestandards.org/ELA-Literacy/SL/2)

* The performance expectations marked with an asterisk integrate traditional science content with engineering through a Practice or Disciplinary Core Idea.

The section entitled "Disciplinary Core Ideas" is reproduced verbatim from *A Framework for K-12 Science Education: Practices, Cross-Cutting Concepts, and Core Ideas* (http://www.nap.edu/catalog.php?record_id=13165). Integrated and reprinted with permission from the National Academy of Sciences.

Figure 8.6 NGSS Lead States. (NGSS Lead States [2013]. Next Generation Science Standards: for states by states. National Academies Press)

The possibilities are endless and allow for teachers to use creative flexibility in their lesson planning and design as well.

It should be noted, however, that the ETS DCIs are not limited to performance expectations where they stand alone; they are also used alongside DCIs from the other scientific disciplines such as in figure 8.7.

Here, you can see that the performance expectation is targeted directly at the fourth grade level and requires the design of a solution to a problem related to Earth processes rather than designing a solution in the abstract.

4-ESS3-2 Earth and Human Activity

Students who demonstrate understanding can:

4-ESS3-2. Generate and compare multiple solutions to reduce the impacts of natural Earth processes on humans.* [Clarification Statement: Examples of solutions could include designing an earthquake resistant building and improving monitoring of volcanic activity.] [Assessment Boundary: Assessment is limited to earthquakes, floods, tsunamis, and volcanic eruptions.]

The performance expectation above was developed using the following elements from the NRC document *A Framework for K-12 Science Education*:

Science and Engineering Practices	Disciplinary Core Ideas	Crosscutting Concepts
Constructing Explanations and Designing Solutions (http://www.nap.edu/openbook.php?record_id=13165&page=67) Constructing explanations and designing solutions in 3–5 builds on K-2 experiences and progresses to the use of evidence in constructing explanations that specify variables that describe and predict phenomena and in designing multiple solutions to design problems. (http://www.nap.edu/openbook.php?record_id=13165&page=67) • Generate and compare multiple solutions to a problem based on how well they meet the criteria and constraints of the design solution. (http://www.nap.edu/openbook.php?record_id=13165&page=67)	**ESS3.B: Natural Hazards** (http://www.nap.edu/openbook.php?record_id=13165&page=192) • A variety of hazards result from natural processes (e.g., earthquakes, tsunamis, volcanic eruptions). Humans cannot eliminate the hazards but can take steps to reduce their impacts. *(Note: This Disciplinary Core Idea can also be found in 3.WC.)* (http://www.nap.edu/openbook.php?record_id=13165&page=192) **ETS1.B: Designing Solutions to Engineering Problems** (http://www.nap.edu/openbook.php?record_id=13165&page=206) • Testing a solution involves investigating how well it performs under a range of likely conditions. (secondary) (http://www.nap.edu/openbook.php?record_id=13165&page=206)	**Cause and Effect** (http://www.nap.edu/openbook.php?record_id=13165&page=87) • Cause and effect relationships are routinely identified, tested, and used to explain change. (http://www.nap.edu/openbook.php?record_id=13165&page=87) -------------------------------------- **Connections to Engineering, Technology, and Applications of Science** **Influence of Engineering, Technology, and Science on Society and the Natural World** (http://www.nap.edu/openbook.php?record_id=13165&page=212) • Engineers improve existing technologies or develop new ones to increase their benefits, to decrease known risks, and to meet societal demands. (http://www.nap.edu/openbook.php?record_id=13165&page=212)

Connections to other DCIs in fourth grade:
4.EST1.C (/4ps4-waves-applications-technologies-information-transfer)

Articulation of DCIs across grade-levels:
K.ETS1.A (/kess3-earth-human-activity) ; 2.ETS1.B (/2ls2-ecosystems-interactions-energy-dynamics) ; 2.ETS1.C (/2ess2-earth-systems) ; MS.ESS2A (/msess2-earth-systems) ; MS.ESS3.B (/msess3-earth-human-activity) ; MS.ETS1.B (/msls2-ecosystems-interactions-energy-dynamics)

Common Core State Standards Connections:

ELA/Literacy -	
RI.4.1 (http://www.corestandards.org/ELA-Literacy/RI/4)	Refer to details and examples in a text when explaining what the text says explicitly and when drawing inferences from the text. (4-ESS3-2) (http://www.corestandards.org/ELA-Literacy/RI/4)
RI.4.9 (http://www.corestandards.org/ELA-Literacy/RI/4)	Integrate information from two texts on the same topic in order to write or speak about the subject knowledgeably. (4-ESS3-2) (http://www.corestandards.org/ELA-Literacy/RI/4)
Mathematics -	
MP.2 (http://www.corestandards.org/Math/Practice/MP2)	Reason abstractly and quantitatively. (4-ESS3-2) (http://www.corestandards.org/Math/Practice/MP2)
MP.4 (http://www.corestandards.org/Math/Practice/MP4)	Model with mathematics. (4-ESS3-2) (http://www.corestandards.org/Math/Practice/MP4)
4.OA.A.1 (http://www.corestandards.org/Math/Content/4/OA)	Interpret a multiplication equation as a comparison, e.g., interpret $35 = 5 \times 7$ as a statement that 35 is 5 times as many as 7 and 7 times as many as 5. Represent verbal statements of multiplicative comparisons as multiplication equations. (4-ESS3-2) (http://www.corestandards.org/Math/Content/4/OA)

* The performance expectations marked with an asterisk integrate traditional science content with engineering through a Practice or Disciplinary Core Idea.

The section entitled "Disciplinary Core Ideas" is reproduced verbatim from *A Framework for K-12 Science Education: Practices, Cross-Cutting Concepts, and Core Ideas* (http://www.nap.edu/catalog.php?record_id=13165). Integrated and reprinted with permission from the National Academy of Sciences.

Figure 8.7 NGSS Lead States. (NGSS Lead States [2013]. Next Generation Science Standards: for states by states. National Academies Press)

A Challenge to Teaching STEM in Science

Though there are a wealth of benefits to teaching using an engineering design model or STEM-based approach, challenges may arise. One is that science and engineering are epistemologically different. In chapter 4 of this textbook, we explored the nature of science and discussed what science is (and isn't). The purpose of science is to better understand the world around us. The inquiry process is one that allows teachers to investigate questions. Engineering, on the other hand, is focused on problem-solving. In the simplest terms, engineers use science and mathematics to solve problems. Understanding these key differences is critical for teachers of young children.

Challenge: Consider the five-step engineering design process alongside the 5E Learning Cycle model. How are they similar and different? Consider what kinds of topics or ideas are best suited for each model.

Imagine a class was studying plant growth and wanted to test the growth of the same type of bean seeds in several different types of soil. The teacher and class would develop a procedure. For example, the students would add 10 mL of water to each plant on Tuesdays and Fridays for three weeks. The students would make daily observations and measure the height of the plants in centimeters on Mondays. Now, what if the students noticed that one type of soil was very dry by Monday morning after the weekend? A scientist would continue following the procedure as written and record the observed dry soil, as the goal of science is to understand the phenomenon. An engineer might create a barrier that prevents water from evaporating or add more water to that soil. The goal of engineering is to solve problems, and the problem that emerged was dry soil. Though science and engineering go hand-in-hand and are often used together, making these differences clear for students is absolutely essential.

Many great teaching resources exist to aid teachers in using STEM effectively and in a way that complements science instruction. Consider the list below as a starting point:

- The NGSS appendix I maps out exactly where and how the engineering design process is integrated into their performance expectations across the curriculum.
- The National Science Teaching Association (NSTA) publishes a teacher journal called *Science and Children* focused on elementary science. This journal features a regular section called "Engineering Encounters" that provides short articles, lessons, and tips for teachers.

- The Boston Museum of Science created a curriculum, *Engineering is Elementary*, that includes a multitude of free resources for teachers available at: eie.org.

STEAM

Soon after STEM rose to popularity, arts-integrated STEM, or STEAM, emerged as a discipline of its own. The inclusion of arts into science or STEM teaching has been well received from many professional organizations such as the National Art Education Association, which states in its position statement that "NAEA believes that to be successful in STEM related career fields, students must be proficient in visual thinking and creative problem-solving facilitated by a strong visual art education." In a similar light, the NGSS emphasizes the importance of the design process in use of design in engineering instruction (appendix J, NRC, 2013e). Research also demonstrates that there are many benefits to STEAM such as increased memory of science content (Hardiman et al., 2019) and more careful observation and "knowing" of scientific phenomena (Iared et al., 2017). Much like the benefits of productive struggle, the time and careful observation that come with art-making can help students to engage deeply with the content they are learning.

However, simply engaging in art-making as an add-on to a science or STEM activity is not the same thing as arts-integrated instruction. For example, writing a rap or drawing a picture at the conclusion of a lesson doesn't include art as a tool for learning or meaning-making. I offer some suggestions for integrating the arts into STEM instruction to activate students' creativity and enhance learning.

In Mrs. Ryan's kindergarten class, children worked in the library with piles of objects for art-making. The students were concluding an activity about waste in which they learned about the differences in compost and recycling. For an assessment, the children were asked to sort objects into the two categories and create collages of natural objects and representations (e.g., pipe cleaners for worms) to visually represent the components of compost. Here, the act of art-making helped the teacher to know which students had a good handle on what was compostable.

Figure 8.8 Children sharing compost collages. (Lauren Madden)

In a recent project, I collaborated with colleagues in art education to create tools for teachers to use when visiting an exhibit on our campus, *Springs Eternal* (Madden et al., in press). The exhibit included works from several artists focused on several characteristics of water—from the liquid we drink to the habitat for microorganisms and many things in between. We identified connections between the artists' work and teaching standards and offered suggestions for using their work in classroom settings. Afterward, we found four key areas for arts integration: communication, community building, content explanation, and creative expression. Thinking about these areas helped us to generate ideas for lessons that were truly interdisciplinary.

Communication

The arts can be used in many ways to communicate information, especially about issues related to the environment and social justice. The image in figure 8.9 of a seal caught in plastic pollution communicates a strong message about pollution that could spark further investigation of human impacts on natural systems.

Other works, such as prints or paintings with explicit messages about science or conservation, are more literal. Students can engage in printmaking to share messages or reflect on the works of others. Music and drama can also be used to "tell the story" of a scientific idea in a way that reaches large masses of people.

Figure 8.9 A seal caught in plastic pollution. (Nels Isrealson)

Community Building

The act of creating art in a classroom space is often collaborative among classmates and can help to build community. When engaging in a design challenge, students might use artistic elements to design things people might want to use. For example, creating a better thermos to carry lunch to school might require a lot of discussion about various visual features and result in a collaborative design. Some works of art are designed to be interactive as well. At Water Bar, a public studio in Minneapolis, visitors taste tap water from many locations and discuss where their water comes from. This helps build community among visitors along with a better understanding of this natural resource.

Figure 8.10 A water-tasting event held by Water Bar Minneapolis. (Lauren Madden)

Content Explanation

The arts can be used to explain science content in a way that words and numbers can't do alone. Take, for example, the piece for string quartet "A Song for Our Warming Planet," which uses climate data from 133 years to determine the pitch of the notes being played by each of the musicians. Though we can look at many complicated graphs of this information, hearing the music allows us to develop a more complete understanding of these trends over time. Creating sculptures of particles at the microscale or nanoscale can also help students to understand the behavior of very small objects in ways that simply viewing models or reading about them cannot.

Creative Expression

One popular way to integrate STEAM into science teaching and learning is through the use of maker spaces. These can take any number of formats from a corner in a library with a selection of materials for children to use to enormous fabrication laboratories with 3D printers and other tools. In these spaces, students can use a variety of materials to build in an open-ended fashion to help develop understanding or solve problems. Students can learn to use plastic bags to knit mats like the one in figure 8.11. Middle

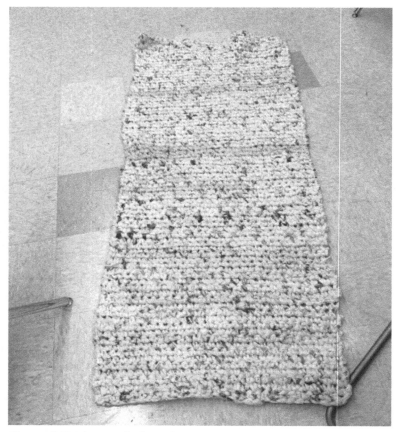

Figure 8.11 Mat made from knitting discarded grocery store bags. (Lauren Madden)

school teacher Morgan Pestorius worked with her school's environmental club to use plastic bags to create these mats and donated them to homeless individuals to use as a sleeping surface. Likewise, students with access to 3D printers can print prosthetic limbs for hurt animals—the possibilities are truly endless and focused on creative thinking.

As you can see, there is great value to integrating across the various STEM disciplines and including the arts in your teaching. But purposeful planning is needed to ensure that productive instruction takes place.

Following this chapter, you'll find an example lesson created by some of my students. They took a field trip to visit the *Springs Eternal* exhibit and were challenged to develop a lesson plan based on this visit. A group of my students enjoyed the work of Marguerita Hagan, which included sculptures of diatoms and other microscopic marine organisms. After the visit, I showed the students images of the diatoms in the lakes in our campus. The students decided to create a fifth grade lesson during which students would walk around the lake and collect trash, then use Hagan's sculptures as inspiration to create sculptures of the diatoms in our campus lake. In this case, the students thought carefully about scale, proportion, and quantity and then used the arts to explain content and express creativity. Using this lesson as inspiration, choose one NGSS performance expectation that integrates DCIs from the ETS category and generate ideas for how you might teach a lesson aligned to that standard. Make sure to consider:

- how science and engineering are different,
- how you might use the engineering design process in your teaching, and
- when you might integrate the arts and what their purpose is in the lesson.

CONCLUSION

In summary, STEM and STEAM can be powerful tools for engaging students in thinking creatively and solving problems. However, it is critical that teachers are purposeful in designing learning experiences that require students to integrate across content areas and not just use technology or arts as "add-ons." Additionally, teachers must be prepared to help students work through struggles as many failed attempts are often part of the engineering design process. When used intentionally, STEM and STEAM can engage and excite students.

CHAPTER 8 SUPPLEMENTARY LESSON:
RIDE OR DIATOM LESSON

Title or Topic of the Lesson and Grade Level: Ride or Diatoms, Fifth Grade

Lesson Essential Question(s):

- What role do microorganisms play in their ecosystems?
- How does human activity affect the microorganisms' ecosystem?

Standards:
NGSS:

> 5-ESS3. Obtain and combine information about ways individual communities use science ideas to protect the Earth's resources and environment.

Learning Objectives and Assessments:

Objectives	Assessments
Students will be able to identify different diatoms and their functions.	In their science notebooks, students will discuss with their peers given different types of diatoms and their functions.
Students will be able to create accurate models of diatoms using household items.	Students will create an accurate model based on their ability to differentiate diatoms.
Students will be able to determine the effects human activity has on the environment, specifically water.	Students will label the different materials used to create the model with the effect they have on our water systems.

Materials:
trash from local water source
sample of water that contains diatoms
glue
tape

Pre-lesson Assignments/Prior Knowledge:

- Students must have visited the *Springs Eternal* exhibit, particularly taking note of Marguerita Hagen's sculptures.
- Students will have observed other organisms, although they may not have been microscopic.
- Students may have knowledge of pollution and its effects on ecosystems.

Lesson Beginning:
Teacher will begin the lesson by asking students what they know and think about the ecosystem in TCNJ lake(s). What might live there? What are the smallest and largest parts? What roles do they play in this ecosystem? They should brainstorm in small groups.

Instructional Plan:

1. The lesson will begin with observing water from TCNJ's lakes, which would be gathered beforehand by the teacher, and looking at the images from the electron microscope that were already taken.
2. Students will look at images of diatoms from TCNJ's lakes and draw an example of those diatoms, a sketch that will later become their physical model. After discussion with their table groups, they will note important things that diatoms do for the water ecosystem, which was discussed in the table groups and among the class.
3. After determining and noting the importance of diatoms in the ecosystem, students will go back to the TCNJ lakes to gather small pieces of garbage that are around the lake. Each student needs to pick up a reasonable amount of safe garbage (not anything dangerous or incredibly dirty) because they will use it in their physical model (small field trip, 30–60 minutes).
4. Students will then take their gathered garbage, look back at their model sketch, and begin to assemble their physical models of diatoms (one or two science blocks over a few days).
5. After completion of the models, students will put the diatoms all together in the classroom or in a display case in the school for everyone to see and explain the significance of diatoms and pollution in our waters.

Differentiation:

- Strategic groupings will be used in order to encourage students who struggle to tap into their creative sides to get out of their comfort zones.
- The teacher will also be readily available to attach certain pieces of materials if the students are struggling.
- If students finish early, they can create a tag for their art piece that provides extra information (what trash is used, where the trash was found, etc.).

Questions:

- If we didn't pick up this trash, what do you think would happen to it? What about the environment that we found it in?
- Is turning this trash into art a form of recycling? Why or why not?
- What other creative/alternative ways of recycling can you think of?
- We have observed our lake's current environment. What other places can you think of that you could collect trash from and recycle in creative ways?
- Who is affected by litter? How and why?

Classroom Management:

- For the groupings, it may be beneficial to include students who like to be hands-on in art-related activities mixed with students who are less inclined to take leadership roles when it comes to building models.
- It would still be very important to have all of the students in the group involved, so give each group member a specific job when it comes to building the model and assembling the materials.
- Some behavioral problems could be that not every student wants to get involved but this can be avoided through the assigning of jobs among the members.
- Another possible behavioral problem is that the students may be more preoccupied with playing with the materials for their model rather than building it. This can be avoided by having the students draw out their ideas for their model before building it to give them direction.

Transitions:
Describe how you will transition and make connections between activities.

After having students explore images of diatoms and having them draw what they saw, we will actually take them to the TCNJ lake to view the ecosystem in which we find these microorganisms. While at the lake, we can discuss with the students strategies to help these small and important organisms survive, like picking up trash that surrounds the lake, which we will then use to make models of the diatoms to share our discoveries with the world.

Closure:
The lesson will end with a mini-lesson on the function of diatoms in an ecosystem. After the mini-lesson students, will complete two anchor charts: "What Do We Know About Diatoms?" and "What Do We Wonder About Diatoms?" These will allow students to make a connection between the mini-lesson and their own models of diatoms.

9
Beginning to Use Science to Advocate

■ ■ ■

In 2019, Greta Thunberg, a Swedish climate activist, made international news advocating for all people to listen to the scientists and act to help mitigate climate change. What made her activism most intriguing was that she is only a teenager, and her voice helped lift other youth activists' work into the public eye.

The other most salient part of Greta's rise in the public eye is that it advocates for an important cause using science. She uses her public persona to leverage data as evidence to support claims and (hopefully) spark action.

In this chapter, we will discuss ways to use science to advocate. We will cover strategies for using science to help support positions and causes. We will also discuss strategies for bringing scientific culture into the classroom and advocating for diverse voices in science.

In order to advocate using science, one must have a good handle on what science is. In chapter 4 of this textbook, I detailed what science *is* and *isn't* and discussed the nature of science at length. Later, I introduced STEM and STEAM in chapter 8 and compared and contrasted science and engineering. As a refresher, science is one way of knowing the world. Through science, data are used as evidence to support or refute claims. This process is called *reasoning*. Scientific theories are ideas about the natural world that have been substantiated through repeated

Figure 9.1 Youth Climate Activist Greta Thunberg. (Anders Hellberg)

experimentation and/or testing. Theories provide mechanisms for processes we observe in the world around us. Scientific laws, on the other hand, simply state what phenomena occur. It bears repeating that science is not about belief. Science simply explains; it does not assert beliefs, whether political, religious, moral, or otherwise.

SCIENTIFIC ARGUMENTATION

One way to advocate using science is through scientific argumentation. One of the science and engineering practices associated with the NGSS is *engaging in argument from evidence*. **Argumentation** is the systematic process of evaluating a claim. But what does that look like in an elementary science lesson? And how can this process of argumentation be used as a tool for advocacy?

In an article targeted at middle school teachers, Bulgren and Ellis (2015) present a framework called the Argumentation Evaluation Strategy (AES) to help students think through the process of linking claims to evidence and evaluating claims and counterclaims. The AES first asks the students to *identify a* **claim** along with **qualifiers** (i.e., stipulations based on time or other factors associated with the claim) to that claim. Next, students list **evidence**. The evidence is then marked as either: **data, fact, opinion,** or **theory**. Students then evaluate the quality of the evidence. Next, the students evaluate the reasoning linking the claim to evidence. Each part of the reasoning is then marked as *authority* (such as research published in credible sources), *theory*, or *logic* (divided further into *analogy, correlation, cause-effect,* or *generalization*). Students then evaluate the quality of the reasoning. Finally, the students decide whether to *accept, reject,* or *withhold judgment* about the argument.

Bulgren and Ellis's work might seem cumbersome for some elementary school teachers and students, especially as the ideas around claims, evidence, and reasoning are fairly new for elementary-aged children. Yet the AES framework could prove to be a helpful tool for elementary school teachers in providing comments while guiding their students and in giving feedback on argumentation. Lee and Hanuscin (2014) offer a simpler approach to structuring scientific argumentation for elementary-aged students. After asking students to identify a claim, support that claim with evidence, and use reasoning to connect the two, students then evaluate one another's claims. These authors suggest using simple sentence starters to scaffold students' critique and analysis of one another's arguments. These were:

- I think you need further evidence because . . .
- I don't think your claim matches your evidence because . . .
- I think you should also consider . . .
- I want to know more about how you . . .
- I don't think your argument is accurate because . . .

Providing these scaffolds for students can help students to think critically when evaluating evidence in a way that can help to generate stronger arguments.

In Mrs. Cornelius's second grade class, her students were making observations of the school's courtyard outdoor classroom in preparation for an improvement project in which more plants, tools, and seating would be added. After the children slowly walked around the courtyard and took notes, she brought them back to the classroom for a whole class discussion about their observations and suggestions for changes.

Mrs. Cornelius asked the group, "What things did you notice that could be used to help us learn more about the weather?" Several students responded with tools such as a weather vane, rain meter, and thermometer. One child added, "The leaves on the trees." Several children in the class shook their heads in disagreement—leaves on a tree were not a tool for learning about weather, at least not in their opinion. Mrs. Cornelius asked the student to provide more evidence for his claim that the leaves on the trees could tell us more about weather. He responded that the leaves would stay wet after rain, move in the wind, change color with different seasons, and fall in the autumn. By asking this child to provide evidence and reasoning, she allowed him to engage in argumentation and support his claim about the tool he noticed.

Challenge: Imagine your school is trying to decide whether to plant vegetables or flowers in a garden bed near the front of the school. Consider one argument your class could make for flowers. What would their claim look like? What could they use for evidence? How could the students structure reasoning to support their claim? What counterarguments might students make to support planting vegetables instead?

SOCIOSCIENTIFIC ISSUES

One strategy for helping students to advocate for science and strengthen their use of argumentation is through introducing socioscientific issues (SSIs) into the classroom. Kahn's 2019 book, *It's Still Debatable! Using Socioscientific Issues to Develop Scientific Literacy*, provides a wealth of tools to help teachers engage students by using debatable and engaging scenarios. The book offers a multitude of lesson examples as well as tools, such as graphic organizers and science trade books, to help structure lessons on SSIs. One example lesson asks first grade students to make an argument whether or not we need zoos. Societal issues such as the rights of animals come to the fore as students consider science content related to habitats, growth and development of organisms, as well as ideas from social studies and language arts like making connections between text and illustration and taking social action. In a lesson designed for fourth graders, students engage in debate about whether distracted walking, or walking while using an electronic device, should be illegal. The SSIs can be used to pique interest in intriguing questions. The SSIs also give children examples of what sort of ideas, causes, and concepts that science can be used for in advocacy work.

CONTROVERSIAL IDEAS IN SCIENCE

Some science topics are frequently the subject of debate, especially by the public and media and often between scientists and nonscientists. Several years ago, I wrote an essay for *The Educational Forum* titled "Teaching Science Is a Sacred Act." In it, I made the argument that it is critical for elementary school teachers, who work each day with children, to understand what is and isn't science. The future citizens and decision makers in our country are sitting in elementary school classrooms today, and it is essential that they develop the tools for evaluating information, separating science from pseudoscience, and making informed decisions based on sound logic and accurate information. Some antiquated nonscientific ideas seem to be held only by fringe groups such as the Flat Earth Society or those who reject the heliocentric model of the universe. However, there are other ideas held by many that you may encounter as a future teacher, and it is necessary to build the appropriate background knowledge and skill set to face these head on.

Take, for example, the idea of human-caused climate change. Through repeated observation, experimentation, and analysis of data, nearly all scientists agree that human-caused climate change is real and a threat to humanity (NASA, 2020). Interestingly, some who make arguments against human-caused climate change often cite the work of Judith Curry, a former scientist and professor at the Georgia Institute of Technology, to support their arguments.[1] Dr. Curry's image and work are often used as a contrast to Greta Thunberg's in memes and stories designed to disparage the teen activist's work. Yet when one reads Dr. Curry's early arguments presented at congressional hearings and published findings, it becomes clear that she did not deny the existence of human-caused climate change at all. Rather, she questioned the mathematical models that scientists use

---

1. For a detailed history of Curry's statements and beliefs, visit Skeptical Science: https://skepticalscience.com/Judith_Curry_art.htm.

and the magnitude of the effect. Her credentials were used by climate change deniers as evidence. As she gained popularity in certain media circles, her own public persona changed and included more questions of human-caused climate change and denial of factual information (e.g., she stated that global warming ceased in 1998 when the highest temperatures on record were observed in the 2010s). Meanwhile, scientific data (e.g., greenhouse gases like carbon dioxide on the rise matching our rise in global temperature) make it clear that human activity is the primary driver of climate change over the past century.

For some teachers, climate change can feel like an extremely touchy subject, leading to discomfort introducing ideas that some in the general public find to be controversial. The most important word of caution when teaching climate change and other controversial topics is to remove belief from the classroom discussion and cover factual information only. Golden and colleagues (2012) offer an interesting strategy in which students use numerical, graphical, photographic, and satellite image data to make a claim whether or not humans are responsible for climate change. In this lesson, students must use only the data to support or refute claims, thus staying away from beliefs of all kinds. If a teacher were to encounter pushback from parents or colleagues, sticking with only data-driven discussions can help decrease any perceived controversy.

Global climate change is a key Disciplinary Core Idea in the NGSS, with performance expectations beginning in middle school. However, there are a multitude of ideas that precede it, such as those relating to the difference between weather and climate and humans' impact on the environment that are covered in the elementary years. For example, the two third grade performance expectations listed below require students to think critically about weather in various regions and how weather and climate differ.

> 3-ESS2-1. Represent data in tables and graphical displays to describe typical weather conditions expected during a particular season.
> 3-ESS2-2. Obtain and combine information to describe climates in different regions of the world.

Again, if faced with pushback from colleagues, parents, or administration, it is essential to use data to drive all discussion and to ensure your teaching is well-aligned with the NGSS at your grade level. It is also essential that elementary teachers feel comfortable in their own understanding of climate change and other potentially controversial topics. Some great tools to help teachers brush up on this important content can be found at the National Education Association.[2] The National Science Teaching Association (NSTA) also provides clear guidance for teachers in its position statement on the teaching of climate science: "The scientific consensus on the occurrence, causes, and consequences of climate change is both broad and deep" (NSTA, 2018a). Like the NEA, the NSTA offers a compilation of resources for K–12 teachers focused on both science content and pedagogy.[3]

Yet climate change is not alone as a topic that some in the general public find controversial while scientists agree on factual information. Vaccine efficacy falls into this category as well. Doctors and scientists agree that vaccines are necessary for eradicating disease and protecting human health. Medical professional groups such as the American Academy of Pediatrics, Centers for Disease Control, and World Health Organization also support their efficacy. Yet some parents choose not to vaccinate children, citing rejected findings and pseudoscience to support their claims. Bronfin (2008) offers an extensive report on the history of the anti-vaxx movement along with the outcomes of actual clinical trials around vaccine use. This article is published in the *Oschner Journal*, a reputable peer-reviewed medical publication that disseminates information in layman's terms. This journal is also a good reference point for teachers seeking to enhance their own content knowledge around a multitude of medical issues before teaching. Topics related to the use of vaccines are introduced as early as first grade when students begin to look for similarities and differences in parents and offspring, such as through the following performance expectation in the NGSS:

1-LS1-2. Read texts and use media to determine patterns in behavior of parents and offspring that help offspring survive.

The Children's Hospital of Philadelphia created an extensive list of lessons at the elementary, middle, and high school levels aligned directly with the NGSS through their Vaccine Makers Project.[4] Though many joke that elementary schools are "germ factories," discussing disease transfer is a relevant and engaging project for children and allows them to connect their science learning to their everyday lives.

Along with climate change and vaccine efficacy, evolution sits as a controversial topic that sometimes leads to discomfort for teachers. The

---

2. http://www.nea.org/climatechange.
3. https://www.nsta.org/climate/.
4. https://vaccinemakers.org/.

topic is so controversial that the NSTA has issued a position statement clearly defining the importance of teaching this topic. As they note, "If evolution is not taught, students will not achieve the level of scientific literacy needed to be well-informed citizens and prepared for college and STEM careers. This position is consistent with that of the National Academies, the American Association for the Advancement of Science (AAAS), and many other scientific and educational organizations" (NSTA, 2013). The NGSS introduce the topic of evolution in third grade through the following performance expectation:

> 3-LS4-1. Analyze and interpret data from fossils to provide evidence of the organisms and the environments in which they lived long ago.

Yet NSTA does not deny that the topic is controversial and offers a lengthy list of tools for teaching across the K–12 spectrum on its resource page.[5] Generally speaking, the best strategy for teaching evolution is the same as that for climate change: remove beliefs from the discussion, present data and factual information, and allow students to support claims with evidence. It might also be helpful to offer examples of scientists with strong religious beliefs who don't find a conflict between evolution and religion such as the Vatican's chief astronomer, Brother Guy Consolmagno. Cartlidge (2015) presents an interview with the Br. Consolmagno that sheds light on the ways in which this astronomer and Jesuit brother uses science to better understand his own world view. In his words: "If you think you already know everything about the world, you are not a good scientist, and if you think you know all there is to know about God, then your religious faith is at fault."

Challenge: generate a list of areas sometimes considered controversial that you've encountered. For each item, identify whether you'd like more information on the topic, an idea or two of how you might plan to approach the topic in your future classroom, or both.

INTRODUCING SCIENCE AND SCIENTISTS TO THE ELEMENTARY CLASSROOM

One way to encourage scientific advocacy in the elementary classroom is to create avenues for engaging with science. Though it can seem like a daunting task to introduce ideas that some see as controversial, there are excellent tools for teachers to use to help demystify science and connect students with the content in a meaningful way.

---

5. https://www.nsta.org/evolution/.

- **Access teacher-friendly tools for enhancing your own science content knowledge as you prepare new lessons and units.** No one is an expert at every topic, but thankfully, there are great tools teachers can use to help enhance their own understanding. The NSTA journal dedicated toward elementary science is called *Science and Children*. In each issue, there is a segment titled "Science 101" that provides a one- to three-page overview on a given topic. These can serve as great refreshers for teachers and help to increase confidence and competence in many science disciplines. Another great resource for adult-level content is the American Association for the Advancement of Science's book *Science for All Americans*, available online.[6] This book, divided into various science topics, provides adult-level scientific information for a general audience. Finally, for some topics, YouTube channels offering short and straightforward explanations of various phenomena are available. *Minute Physics*[7] and *Minute Chemistry*[8] provide one- to three-minute explanations for a wide range of topics, such as gravity or how waves work.
- **Bring real science and scientists into your classroom.** In a best-case scenario, a teacher could bring in a practicing scientist from a local business or university to share how his or her research connects to the topics children are studying in school. However, this scenario comes with many logistical and practical implications. This is a time when technology can be used to enhance a classroom experience. Many scientists use Twitter to share their research and findings—and those at universities often feature the great work of the young people who help out in their labs. For example, Dr. Benny Chan, a chemist at The College of New Jersey, showcases his research in figure 9.2.

Notice the hashtags used in Dr. Chan's tweet. These terms are easily searchable and can be helpful for teachers searching for certain topics. There are many other electronic platforms that teachers can use to bring current and exciting works of scientists into their classrooms. Muir (2019) suggests using TikToks to bring science to teens by sharing short videos of interesting phenomena and organisms. These can be just as exciting and useful for young children as well.

---

6. http://www.project2061.org/publications/sfaa/online/sfaatoc.htm.
7. https://www.youtube.com/user/minutephysics.
8. https://www.youtube.com/channel/UCpex4hFTn5GUSDPNZgpRF9g.

← Tweet

 **Benny Chan**
@drbennyc   •••

Look at me... a solid state materials chemist doing green microwave organic reactions on a Saturday! Only a few more student CURE reactions next week to go!
#tcnjinorganic! #tcnjchemistry #tcnjscience

1:05 PM · Nov 2, 2019 · Twitter for iPhone

23 Likes

Figure 9.2 Dr. Benny Chan shares his research on Twitter. (Benny Chan)

Podcasts are also a great tool for breaking down scientific ideas and using storytelling to help engage students with content. On *Wow in the World*,[9] "hosts Mindy Thomas and Guy Raz guide curious kids and their grown-ups on a journey into the wonders of the world around them. We'll go inside our brains, out into space and deep into the coolest new stories in science and technology." Each of these episodes focuses on a topic of interest for students, such as how spicy food works or what exactly black holes are. Another great podcast source for interesting scientific ideas is *Radiolab*.[10] Though this podcast is designed for an adult audience, the scientific storytelling can be exciting for all audiences.

Finally, *Skype a Scientist*[11] is a donation-based program that allows teachers to bring scientists into their classrooms via video or text-based chats.

- **Research topics and issues that are important to your students.** When we think back to the work of educational theorists such as Piaget and Vygotsky discussed in chapter 2 of this book, one clear commonality was the suggestion to build off of students' own knowledge and interests. When a student voices an idea that is scientific in nature, teachers can encourage further curiosity and exploration. Ava DeLeo, a first grader recently in Ms. Alyssa Bloomberg's class at Benjamin Franklin Elementary School in Lawrenceville, New Jersey, was concerned about the number of plastic water bottles she saw in her school's recycling bin. When she told Ms. Bloomberg about her concerns, it sparked a school-wide project focused on reduction of plastics. Children in older grades researched the broader environmental impact of her work while Ava's class stuck to tallying and graphing the number of bottles and creating posters to advocate for reusable bottles. This meaningful project helped all the Benjamin Franklin children connect directly to science and better understand an important issue in their school.

A SENSE OF PLACE

Ava's project was especially meaningful because it connected science to students' interest as well as to their place. "*Place-based learning* engages students in their community, including their physical environment, local

---

9. https://www.npr.org/podcasts/510321/wow-in-the-world.
10. https://www.wnycstudios.org/podcasts/radiolab.
11. https://www.skypeascientist.com/.

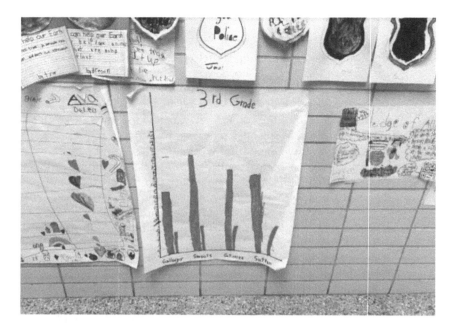

Figure 9.3 Graphs created by students to document plastic bottles collected in recycling bins over time, along with images of bins decorated by students. (Lauren Madden)

culture, history, or people. With place-based learning, students get to see the results of their work in their community. They build communication and inquiry skills, learn how to interact with any environment, and gain a better understanding of themselves, as well as their place in the world" (Hood River Middle School, 2015). Many topics lend themselves easily to place-based learning, specifically those related to better understanding the living and nonliving features of ecosystems, weather patterns, and geological features in a given area. Centering learning in a geographical place can also help students to know more about scientific enterprise in their towns and notable scientists doing that work.

Citizen science is another way to connect students with science and their place. Citizen scientists are often nonexperts who aid and assist in wide-scale scientific endeavors by collecting data on specific projects to share with scientists doing research. On the New Jersey shore, citizen scientists help measure signs of erosion by recording and photographing observations made at various locations through the Paddle for the Edge project.[12] Similarly the Cornell Ornithology lab engages classrooms in documenting birds that visit feeders to help them to track migration.[13] These kinds of projects benefit students and science alike by allowing for active and authentic participation in important research studies.

Sometimes, place can be even more specific *within* a school. In schools with maker spaces, nature trails, or science labs, students could be more likely to engage with the subject than they do in their class-rooms. Oftentimes a place can conjure images of actions and behaviors for children—labs are for *doing* science! One way to help students connect with science is to use a certain arrangement of desks or tables and announce when science time has begun. Another is to have a class set of lab coats available for children. Carrier and colleagues (2020) studied the idea of *enclothed cognition* in elementary-aged students wearing lab coats during science lessons. These authors found that the simple act of putting on the lab coat led to higher science self-efficacy in children. This idea is similar to the teacher adage that children are best behaved on picture day when dressed nicely. On a similar note, Deborah Lee Rose provides a multitude of photographs of all kinds of scientists in her book *Scientists Get Dressed*, from glaciologists to astronauts, to demonstrate the many different ways scientists can look and perhaps help teachers in helping students to assume the role of scientist in their classrooms.

---

12. https://www.barnegatbaypartnership.org/protect/restoring-barnegat-bay/volun teer/paddle-for-the-edge/.

13. https://feederwatch.org/.

Challenge: use a search engine to identify citizen science projects near where you live. Which ones might you use with your future students and why?

CONCLUSION

Understanding science content is critical for all citizens and teachers especially, as they are the most essential contributors to developing a scientifically literate populace. For scientific topics that can be sometimes viewed as controversial, it is especially critical for teachers to (1) develop a solid understanding of the content, (2) encourage scientific argumentation connecting claims to evidence, and (3) stick to fact-based discussions rather than beliefs or opinions. Teachers can support their own work teaching these topics using the resources and position statements developed by professional groups such as the NSTA and NEA. In order to advocate for science and help students to *use* science for advocacy, teachers can use technology to its best advantage. Connecting students to scientists all over the world can give them the tools to better understand their own place and explore their own scientific questions and endeavors. Helping children to carefully observe their own school, community, and ecosystem in a scientific manner can build a sense of wonder and curiosity.

10

Equity, Diversity, and Inclusion in Science Teaching

∎ ∎ ∎

Equality | Equity

Figure 10.1 Equity versus equality. (CC Image courtesy of MPCA on Flickr)

To value and respect the experiences that all students bring from their backgrounds, it is important to make diversity visible. In the process of making diversity visible, there are both connections and disconnections between home/community and classroom/school. Effective teachers understand how disconnections may vary among different student groups, as well as how to capitalize on connections. These teachers bridge diverse students' background knowledge and experiences to scientific knowledge and practices.

—Next Generation Science Standards, appendix D

The statement above offers a vision for science teaching that engages all learners. In this chapter, I will discuss strategies to help realize this vision. But what does an equitable vision for science teaching and learning look like? How do we ensure we are meeting the needs of all students in our science classes?

This chapter will address issues of equity, diversity, and inclusion in science teaching. We will cover some historical context around inequities in science and other STEM disciplines. Next, we'll address strategies for creating more equitable environments through family engagement, purposeful discussion of vocabulary, anti-racist science teaching, and assets-based science teaching. Finally, we'll cover issues related to ability in science teaching and learning and Universal Design for Learning, a strategy for inclusive teaching.

DIVERSITY IN SCIENCE AND ENGINEERING

Bell and Bang (2015) offer some guidance on why equity matters in science education: "Students from non-dominant communities often face *opportunity gaps* in their educational experience. Inclusive approaches to science instruction can reposition youth as meaningful participants in science learning and recognize their science-related assets and those of their communities." These long-standing opportunity gaps have serious consequences. The National Science Foundation released a report in 2015 titled *Women, Minorities, and People with Disabilities in Science and Engineering*, and it reveals some stark contrasts between the population of individuals in STEM professions and those in the general public within the United States.

For example, consider the images in the two pie charts in figure 10.2. On the left, we see the makeup of the population of the US, divided by race and gender, while on the right, we see the population of individuals employed in science or engineering professions, divided by race and gender.

As can be seen so clearly by these graphs, the people who work in science and engineering fields look vastly different from those in the general public. Scientists are whiter and more male than the rest of us. This lack of representation can be devastating and could lead some children to shy away from science because they cannot see themselves in these roles. A recent study at Johns Hopkins University demonstrated that Black children from low-income backgrounds who had just one Black teacher in

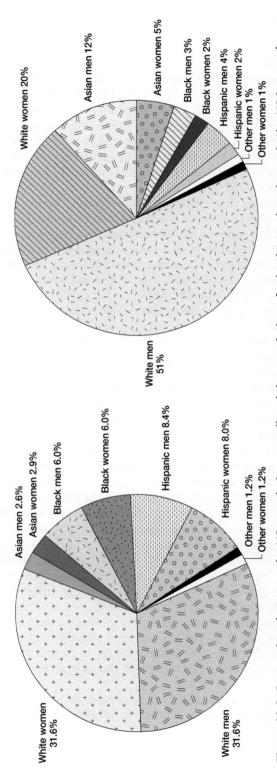

Figure 10.2 Comparison between the US population overall and the population of scientists and engineers in the US by race/ethnicity and gender based on the 2015 NSF Report, *Women, Minorities, and People with Disabilities in Science and Engineering.*

elementary school were significantly more likely to graduate from high school and enroll in college (Rosen, 2018). This idea of representation, or seeing those who look like us, allows us to see ourselves in those kinds of positions. Other studies also show that female children who show interest in science by age ten often lose interest steeply by age fourteen (Archer et al., 2015). A recent Microsoft study in Europe found similar results. Girls' interest in science spiked around age eleven, then dropped sharply by fifteen (Petroff, 2017).

So what can we, as teachers of elementary-aged children, do to help the children in our classrooms see themselves in science? One strategy is to show children diverse representations of science and scientists. In chapter 9 of this book, I showed an example of a scientist's Twitter feed to help connect children to scientific enterprise. To expand on this example, we can make sure to provide a diverse and inclusive vision of science and scientists by highlighting the work of women and scientists of color. Students who can see themselves represented in the discipline, especially by those discovering and creating exciting new things, are more likely to consider career paths in the STEM disciplines themselves. It is equally important to represent scientists as both real and human. In figure 10.3, herpetologist Earyn McGee shows an example of a lizard in a houseplant on her Twitter feed while celebrating the start of Black History Month, a post that could easily be shared in a classroom environment.

It might go without saying, but another way to ensure science is equitable is to engage all students with science. The children in our classrooms deserve a chance to explore scientific questions and engage with phenomena of interest in the outside world. One strategy for connecting students with interesting scientific endeavors is to participate in a citizen science project, similar to those introduced in the previous chapter of this book. Citizen science is a process by which volunteers, who often are not employed as scientists, contribute to data collection on large-scale science projects. These can range in scope and subject and allow for ongoing or one-time contributions by volunteers. Citizenscience.gov provides a comprehensive list of these projects across the United States and offers instructions for getting involved. For example, the Urban Heat Island Mapping project employs the help of hundreds of individuals in recording temperatures across Washington, D.C.; Baltimore, Maryland; and Richmond, Virginia; to create heat maps of these cities.[1] In a different project, Biodiversity Discovery and Phenology in Acadia National Park, volunteers help to identify and track plant and animal species throughout

---

1. https://research.noaa.gov/article/ArtMID/587/ArticleID/2385/High-temperatures-bring-citizen-scientists-to-map-the-hottest-places-in-Baltimore-and-DC.

← **Tweet**

Earyn McGee, Lizard lassoer, MSc 🦎 🌐

@Afro_Herper

I made the pot, potted the plant, then I had to #FindThatLizard

Happy first day of Black History Month y'all. Don't forget support and hire Black people everyday!

5:38 PM · Feb 1, 2021 · Twitter for iPhone

14 Retweets   **281** Likes

Figure 10.3 Herpetologist Earyn McGee's Twitter post. (Earyn McGee)

Acadia National Park.[2] Some citizen science projects require only a computer to participate. For example, Snapshot Safari employs the help of volunteers to identify sightings of animals on cameras installed at various locations across Africa.[3] These kinds of projects help children situate their own place and contribution in the scientific world.

FAMILY ENGAGEMENT

Another tool teachers can employ to create a diverse and inclusive scientific experience for their students is family engagement. Yet it can sometimes be a struggle to bring parents or other family members to school for assemblies and classroom visits, especially when parents might be shift workers or work multiple jobs. Wenner and Galaviz (2020) suggest teachers can occasionally send home "science packs." These are backpacks that teachers pack up with the instructions and materials to complete a science activity at home. Though the authors caution that this process can be time consuming for teachers and parents alike, it creates a link between school and home and allows students to connect science to their own families. Some suggestions to make it easier is to employ student leaders in helping to create the backpacks and limit them to two or three times a year. A simpler strategy is to ask parents or families to help students create entries in a daily weather or moon log. These kinds of everyday observations of the world around us can help students view their family members as scientific.

Equitable science teaching allows students to see science in their lives as well as themselves in science. And, through using science, students can better understand the diverse world in which we live. For example, Long (2019) offers strategies for critically questioning terminology in biology lessons with an eye for inclusivity. One suggestion is to use the terms "egg and sperm" rather than "mother and father" when discussing who contributes genes to offspring. This language can help students who are adopted or part of blended families to better understand their own experiences. Long also cautions about using terms like "conditions" rather than "disorders" and describing mutations as changes, rather than mistakes, in a genetic code. These small changes in the language we use allow children to understand science as an inclusive practice that can and should include them. Similarly, it is critical that we don't reserve discussions of diverse scientists for the "special" months such as Black History or Women's History months.

---

2. https://schoodicinstitute.org/.
3. https://www.zooniverse.org/organizations/meredithspalmer/snapshot-safari.

Another suggestion is to use a multicultural approach to science teaching more broadly. In the *Encyclopedia of Science Education*, Mensah (2015) offers the following definition for multiculturalism with respect to science teaching:

> Multiculturalism is a philosophical position and movement that assumes that the gender, ethnic, racial, and cultural diversity of a pluralistic society should be reflected in all of its institutionalized structures but especially in educational institutions, including the staff, norms and values, curriculum, and student body. It recognizes that equality and equity are not the same thing, meaning that equal access does not necessarily guarantee fairness.

Several years ago, I visited a second grade class covering plant structure and function. Many of the children in the class were of Indian Hindu descent. When the teacher asked the class, "What are leaves for?" a little boy responded that he didn't know but Hindus believed that the leaves are where plants made their food. Rather than incorporate the student's home perspective into the class discussion, the teacher moved on. A colleague and I offered some other suggestions for integrating the scientific and cultural beliefs of this child in a class discussion instead, to allow for the student to see himself better represented in his class and in science at large, using a multicultural perspective (Madden & Joshi, 2013).

ANTI-RACIST SCIENCE TEACHING

Scholars largely agree that simply rejecting racism is not the same thing as taking an anti-racist perspective. As Dr. Bettina Love (2021) stated, anti-racist work in schools "needs instead to embed community efforts, organizers, and the actual people who live with America's oppression. It needs to make structural changes that dismantle centuries-old, racist institutions from the ground up in order to rebuild with a commitment to community, safety (without police), justice, diversity, and actual equity. For equity work to work, it must be handed to the community." Davis and Tiller Smith (2020) offer guidance for teachers implementing an anti-racist perspective into elementary science teaching. Their suggestions include (1) evaluating curriculum and reading materials and modifying them to ensure they include historical and cultural figures from a diverse range of backgrounds, (2) modifying instructional strategies to include more student voices and a variety of methods to meet the needs of the diverse body of students in a given classroom, and (3) building relationships with others to help leverage the voices of students and scientists from a variety of backgrounds to ensure the science curriculum is relevant and representative.

SCIENTIFIC VOCABULARY

There are a multitude of perspectives on when and how to introduce content area vocabulary; this is true in science and all other disciplines. Scientific language can be confusing and overly complicated, and this level of difficulty can be a barrier to many children in learning science. Lindahl (2019) asks the following four questions before she introduces new terminology:

1. Will this word help students as they think about and discuss the ideas in that unit?
2. Will they have enough opportunities to practice speaking the word for it to become a part of their functional vocabulary?
3. Will it show up again later on in the school year?
4. Is not knowing this word a barrier to accessing material they will use for learning?

If she answers no to any of the questions above, she carefully considers how and why she would introduce a complicated term. When she does introduce these terms, Lindahl uses multiple modes such as verbal repetition, drawing, diagramming, and valuing both everyday and scientific language in class conversations. These strategies can allow a student to sense a lower "vocabulary hurdle" when engaging in science.

Several years ago, I was working with a team of prekindergarten teachers on strategies for incorporating more science into their preschool classrooms. One of the first strategies I offered was familiar to the group and disheartened them (to my surprise). I suggested using everyday language as much as possible to help connect to student lives. Apparently, at an earlier training, these teachers received the same advice and altered their science lessons to focus on the idea of comparing. They chose the skill of comparison because the word "compare" was very similar in English and Spanish and would be something they could use to connect to English Language Learners and their parents. However, *compare* in everyday life means to look for differences. When we comparison shop at the grocery store, we look for differences in cost, calories, and nutrients to make informed decisions. Yet in science *compare* means to look for similarities rather than differences. This group of teachers used the everyday term, and when their students were assessed at the end of the school year, they did an outstanding job identifying differences in items but called this process comparing instead of *contrasting*. Sadly, vocabulary is much easier to assess than process and content, and as teachers, we owe it to our students to ensure they are on the right track in terms of use of appropriate scientific language.

Some teachers of English Language Learners find science to be an excellent place to begin inclusive dual language instruction. I once spent time in a bilingual (English and Spanish) second grade class, and the teacher, who was an ELL herself raised by Polish immigrants, found science to be the easiest subject to teach in a bilingual format. She noted that the heavy vocabulary load, especially terms with Latin or Greek roots, tends to be a struggle for English and Spanish speakers alike and provides a place for all students to struggle productively together to better name the processes they engage with in class.

AN ASSETS-BASED APPROACH TO SCIENCE

Often unknowingly, many individuals approach issues around equity and diversity with a *deficit perspective*. Volk and Long (2005) describe this perspective as one that "attributes many children's school failures to perceived deficits within the children, their families, and their cultures." As a result, biases (both explicit and implicit) can color a teacher's perspective on her students' ability to be successful. In contrast, I propose approaching the teaching of science from an *assets-based perspective*. "In the simplest terms, an asset-based approach focuses on strengths. It views diversity in thought, culture, and traits as positive assets. Teachers and students alike are valued for what they bring to the classroom rather than being characterized by what they may need to work on or lack" (NYU, 2018). To return to the example of the little boy who shared his cultural knowledge about plant growth, imagine how a teacher could use this cultural knowledge as an asset rather than something to move past. What suggestions would you make to position the child's cultural knowledge about plants as an asset?

Another strategy for using an assets-based approach to science teaching is to focus on science process skills and practices that are used in everyday life and draw direct connections to science content presented in classroom settings. Thinking back to the confusion with the skills of compare and contrast the prekindergarten teachers mentioned, we could find some ways to reframe these discussions as assets. For example, a teacher could praise the ways children and their families use the skill of contrasting in everyday life before introducing the difference between compare and contrast in science.

Challenge: imagine your class includes a student who spends a lot of time in the kitchen cooking with his grandmother. How can you use this cooking experience as an asset in your teaching? What about a child who excels in basketball? How might you use her ability to perfect a three-point shot as an asset in science teaching?

SCIENCE TEACHING AS AN INCLUSIVE PRACTICE

Inclusion is a common practice across K–12 educational settings and refers to the concept of placing children who require special education services alongside their more typical peers for all or most of the school day. Inclusion classes are sometimes team-taught: a general education teacher is partnered with a special education teacher, sometimes with the help of paraprofessionals or teacher assistants. Other times, inclusion classes are taught by just one teacher with training in special education. Inclusive classrooms sometimes provide children who require special education services the *least restrictive environment* for learning, allowing these children to work alongside their peers for more of the school day. As a result, teachers must consider the needs of learners with a broad range of backgrounds, knowledge, and abilities. In classrooms that aren't designated *inclusion*, teachers might have larger class sizes during science lessons, as most children with diagnosed disabilities receive extra support or "pull out" time for English language arts or mathematics. So elementary teachers are challenged with the following question: how can we structure science lessons to meet the needs of all students, including those with special needs? Finson and colleagues (2011) offer a handbook of practical strategies for modifying science materials with specific learning needs in mind, but in this chapter, we will offer some overall guidance on inclusive practices in designing science learning activities overall.

Universal Design for Learning

Universal Design for Learning (UDL) is considered a best practice for all educators and was developed in the 1980s by the Center for Applied Special Technology (CAST) to help teachers develop flexible curricular materials (CAST, 2018). Inspired by universal design in architecture, teaching and learning inspired by UDL includes elements that are necessary for some but helpful for many. A common example of a universal design element in architecture is a sidewalk ramp. While it is necessary for individuals in wheelchairs, it is also helpful for people pushing strollers or riding bicycles.[4]

---

4. For a more comprehensive overview on UDL, view this video: https://www.you tube.com/watch?v=bDvKnY0g6e4&feature=youtu.be.

Figure 10.4 Sidewalk ramps are common features of universal design in architecture. (Lauren Madden)

In an educational context, UDL considers the broad range of needs children in a given class might have. First, teachers set goals. Next, they consider the barriers to reaching those goals and use the three principles of UDL to help overcome these barriers. These three principles are: *representation*, *action and expression*, and *engagement*.

Representation: use multiple media and supports to present content. For example, use diagrams and videos alongside traditional text and highlight key information. This includes addressing challenging vocabulary and activating prior knowledge.

Action and Expression: give students multiple models for how they can show what they know and provide support, examples, and feedback frequently.

Engagement: provide options for students to engage, acknowledging that not every child's interest will be sparked by the same phenomenon.

Employing UDL in science teaching may require some shifting of expectations on the part of the teacher. If you're working with the

Brain network	UDL principle
Affective network The "why" of learning	Engagement Provide multiple and flexible means of engaging the learner in what is to be learned so that all students will be motivated to learn. For example, some students work on a project individually, while others, who are stimulated by collaboration, work in teams.
Recognition network The "what" of learning	Representation Provide multiple and flexible means of representing what is to be learned (representation) so that students will be able to access the content of the curriculum. For example, some students may read a textbook, while others use a digital version of the text that includes text-to-speech software.
Strategic network The "how" of learning	Action and expression Provide multiple and flexible means of action and expression so that all students will be able to demonstrate what they have learned. For example, students write their ideas using pens, a keyboard, text to speech, or graphic organisers. Students can demonstrate their understandings by making a video, performing a play, or writing an essay.

Figure 10.5 Framework for using UDL in a classroom to modify instruction.

following NGSS performance expectation,[5] you may have a learning goal or objective that the fifth grade students will use a magnifying glass to observe particles of salt and sugar and to use the property of shape to sort and name these two substances based on this property.

5-PS1-3. Make observations and measurements to identify materials based on their properties.

Representation could be addressed here by defining the terms "particle," "substance," "matter," and "observation." A teacher could also activate prior knowledge by asking students to describe what they already know about salt and sugar.

Engagement could be addressed in this example by providing multiple ways for students to record their observations through words, drawings, or graphic organizers.

Action and expression could be addressed by allowing students to verbally explain their claims on the identity of the substances or do so using a text or diagram-based format.

Challenge: return to the performance expectation above, *5-PS1-3. Make observations and measurements to identify materials based on their properties*. Identify another goal, barriers to that goal, and ways to employ UDL principles to teach this content.

The NSF report on *Women, Minorities, and Persons with Disabilities in Science and Engineering* suggests that people with disabilities are just as likely as the general public to enroll in undergraduate programs in science and engineering. However, these individuals are statistically more likely to be unemployed (NSF, 2015). Using practices such as UDL to structure lessons can help teachers engage these individuals early and help them to identify with science and thrive in these careers.

Thinking back to chapter 2 of this text, we can draw some clear connections between the theorists and strategies for equitable and inclusive science teaching. Vygotsky's idea of scaffolds can provide supportive representations of all sorts of ideas in science. Piaget's focus on prior knowledge can be used to celebrate students' assets and approach instruction that builds off of things they already know. Taken together, this chapter provides ideas and suggestions for making science teaching inclusive and equitable. Through purposeful attention to the needs of students and barriers to addressing those needs, we can provide multiple pathways to engage all students in learning science together.

---

5. It should be noted that this is an example of one activity related to this performance expectation and not an exhaustive approach to covering the entire PE.

CONCLUSION

This chapter addresses the need for equity, diversity, and inclusion in science teaching. There are many strategies for overcoming opportunity gaps experienced by many children including using a multicultural or anti-racist perspective, purposeful introduction of vocabulary, and engaging families in science. Purposefully planning lessons and units with Universal Design for Learning in mind ensures that learners from many backgrounds with a range of abilities can access and participate in science.

11

How Do We Know What We Know in Science?

■ ■ ■

The more you teach without finding out who understands the concepts and who doesn't, the greater the likelihood that only already-proficient students will succeed.

—Grant Wiggins

Though it can sometimes sound like a dirty word, assessment is an essential component of all teaching and learning. In this chapter, I will discuss the landscape of assessment in the US and describe the two key categories of assessment: summative, or assessment to determine value or worth, and formative, or assessment to inform future instruction. In prior chapters, this textbook covered ideas directly related to assessment. In chapter 5, we discussed the history of science standards in the US, while in chapter 6, we provided some guidance on planning lessons—including tools for writing meaningful, behavioral learning objectives. In order to assure our instruction is aligned with NGSS and other standards and that our objectives are met, we necessarily must think purposefully about assessment.

This chapter provides an overview of assessment in general. We discuss types of and purposes for assessment. We discuss summative and formative assessment and provide examples of several types of assessment that can be useful in elementary science.

Reynolds and colleagues (2009) define *assessment* as "any systematic procedure for collecting information that can be used to make inferences about the characteristics of people or objects." In education, assessment is an ongoing process that can be both obvious and hidden to students. Oftentimes the words *assessment* and *testing* are used interchangeably. A *test* is the device or procedure used to obtain information about an individual, and often that information has to do with her behavior, knowledge, or ability in a given context. There are many different types of tests used in educational settings, and each serves a different purpose. It should be clear, however, that tests give teachers information about a sample of what students know and do not provide a full picture of any given student's aptitude or ability alone.

Maximum performance tests measure the upper limits of a test-taker's ability or knowledge. For example, *speed tests* are a type of maximum performance test that assess how quickly a person can complete a type of task. "Mad minutes" measuring completion of arithmetic facts in math lessons or word-per-minute tests for typists fall into this category. On the flip side, *power tests* provide a test-taker with an unlimited amount of time and allow an individual to demonstrate how much they know or understand about a given topic. Qualifying or comprehensive exams in graduate school often fall into this category of maximum performance test. *Achievement tests* are often given after students complete a course or unit while *aptitude tests* are used to predict future performance. End-of-unit tests fall into the category of achievement tests. Aptitude tests can include *placement tests*, which aid teachers in placing students in the appropriate class or level, or *diagnostic tests*, which help teachers determine strengths and areas for assistance (Reynolds et al., 2009). Tests to determine which students might participate in an enrichment program or remediation are considered aptitude tests.

Standardized tests are administered, scored, and interpreted in a standardized manner in order to make comparisons among large groups of students. Many standardized tests are periodically given to a *standardization sample*, or subset of test-takers. The scores of this sample are used to set *norms*, which are patterns of outcomes on that test. The scores of the standardization sample are laid out graphically, and future test-takers' outcomes are then compared to the norms established by the standardization sample. Most often, these scores fall on a bell curve, as shown in figure 11.1. Standardized tests given in this manner are sometimes called *norm-referenced tests*.

Another type of standardized test is a *criterion-referenced test*. In criterion-referenced tests, test-takers' scores are compared to specific criteria rather than other test-takers' scores or outcomes. Regardless of format,

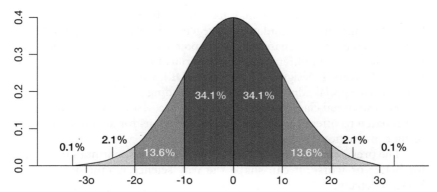

Figure 11.1 Example of a bell curve used to set norms on a standardized test.

standardized tests become *high-stakes tests* when their outcomes have direct consequences for schools, teachers, or students, such as ranking, funding, or parental choice in student placement (Reynolds et al., 2009).

When we think about standardized tests, things like the SAT or GRE often come to mind. What do these have to do with science teaching and learning in particular? No Child Left Behind (NCLB), President George W. Bush's seminal educational reform effort that included reinstating the Elementary and Secondary Education Act (ESEA), required major changes to the US educational system. One such change was to require high-stakes testing in *science* at the fourth, eighth, and twelfth grade levels and to stipulate that these scores would count toward determinations whether schools made Adequate Yearly Progress or AYP (Johnson & Hanegan, 2006). NCLB also mandated that 95 percent of all students were tested alongside their peers. This 95 percent includes students with limited English proficiency and students with special needs. Some other key legislation teachers should be aware of is the Individuals with Disabilities Education Act (IDEA) of 2004, which states that students diagnosed with certain types of disabilities are entitled to a *free and appropriate public education* (FAPE) and must be placed in the least restrictive learning environment. Individuals on schools' child study teams help teachers to develop an *individualized education plan* (IEP) for students with these documented disabilities and outline specific strategies teachers must use with these students. This means that teachers may be required to modify materials, provide additional tools, or work with colleagues and paraprofessionals to ensure that their students' accommodations are being met. Section 504 of the Rehabilitation Act of 1973 defines disability more broadly than IDEA did and allows for students with disabilities not covered in IDEA to receive targeted and specific educational accommodations. *504 plans* are similar to IEPs and provide guidance for teachers in planning and modifying instructional plans and materials. In chapter 10 of this text, I covered several strategies for modifying science materials for use in inclusive settings through Universal Design for Learning (UDL). Given that many students who receive special education services in reading and mathematics are in a more traditional classroom setting for science, elementary teachers must be prepared to offer appropriate accommodations for all students during science instruction.

The prevalence of high-stakes testing in science continues today, and for better or worse, it can shape the way science is taught across the K–12 spectrum.

Recall the previous chapter in this book when we discussed the difference between the everyday and scientific definitions of the term *compare*. Assessing the definition of this term in science can be easily achieved with a simple multiple choice question. Yet is that sort of simple definition of one scientific skill, absent of content or context, helping to build meaningful science learning opportunities for children? Though the skill of comparison is essential for nearly all the NGSS science practices, and in turn, every content domain in science, knowing its definition does not provide meaningful evidence that an individual can use this skill to *do* science. Research demonstrates that students whose teachers employ inquiry-based instruction rather than rote memorization or test preparation–focused instruction score as high as or higher on science standardized tests (e.g., Falk & Drayton, 2004; Geier et al., 2008). Though it might sound counterintuitive, the best way to prepare students to excel on these formal high-stakes tests is to use an inquiry-based approach in the classroom. But this begs the question: how do teachers measure whether their students have mastered science content?

TEACHER-CREATED ASSESSMENT

As we discussed earlier, assessment can be ongoing and sometimes even invisible to students. In today's era of educational accountability, teachers must be able to provide evidence and reasoning for the grades earned by their students. What follows in this next section is an overview of strategies for teacher-created assessment items, which typically assess students summatively.

Selected-Response Items

As the name suggests, selected-response items require a student to select one answer from a choice of several or many. Formats such as multiple choice, matching, and fill-in-the-blank with a word bank fall into the category of selected-response items. Some benefits of using this approach are that selected-response items are simple and quick to grade, as there is, ideally, just one correct answer, and that they provide "apples to apples" comparisons between and among children in the class. Some drawbacks are that they can encourage rote memorization, and it can be challenging to assess higher-order thinking using this approach. It should be noted that while multiple choice questions can encourage rote memorization or learning test-taking strategies over critical thinking, this is not always the case. It is possible to assess higher-order thinking and skills using multiple choice items so long as the test-maker can develop plausible and reasonable distractors (incorrect choices) and the test-taker has sufficient reading and/or mathematical skills to differentiate between the choices.

Strategies for writing effective selected-response items include:

- Avoid clues in your answer or stem. Mirroring phrasing from the correct answer can allow students to respond to these items using test-taking skills rather than their understanding of the content.
- Make distractors appear plausible. Distractors are the incorrect responses in multiple choice items. It can be tempting to include goofy choices that are easy to eliminate, but relying instead on common misconceptions or frequently heard student comments can ensure that your items are measuring what your students know or have learned.
- Limit the use of "always" and "never" answers. Inevitably, each classroom has a student in it who knows the exception to many patterns and rules.
- Ensure responses are of similar length. One test-taking skill students often master is to look for an answer that stands out as different from the others, much like the old *Sesame Street* game, "One of these things is not like the others."
- Use approximately equal numbers of true and false items. Students shouldn't use assessment as a chance to figure out how their teachers are tricking them. Keeping a similar number of responses in each category helps to avoid this assumption.
- Keep all matching items on the same page. The process of constantly flipping pages can be frustrating and ultimately assesses a student's ability to flip pages and not content knowledge.

Constructed-Response Items

When a student is provided with a more open-ended prompt, the assessment is taking a constructed-response format. These types of items can use many different formats ranging from short-answer written responses to longer essays or diagrams. These types of assessments can access students' higher-order thinking skills and allow for students to showcase their creativity. They are also relatively simple to write. On the flip side, it is more challenging to grade these kinds of items objectively.

Strategies for writing effective constructed-response items include:

- Give students grading criteria such as checklists or rubrics in advance. We will discuss suggestions for creating these kinds of grading guides and criteria later in this chapter.
- For short-answer items, make sure there is only one correct response! Students can be incredibly creative and asking a simple question such as, "Water is a _____," can yield a multitude of correct answers ranging from "compound" or "liquid" to "word" or "beverage."
- Make decisions about neatness early—will it count? Let the students know! Some teachers like to include grammar, mathematical conventions, spelling, or neatness as a single category in a grading scale while others choose to assess only science content through science assessments. Your instructional decisions need to be clear to your students before they are assessed.

Portfolio or Performance Assessments

This is by far the most open-ended category and can be the most challenging to grade. These assessments can allow for students to represent ideas in a way that they feel best suits the assignment and can be used to assess skills and content at the same time. As a result, teachers using the NGSS to guide their science instruction might be drawn to performance assessments. Consider the second grade NGSS performance expectation below:

2-ESS2-2. Develop a model to represent the shapes and kinds of land and bodies of water in an area.

In order to assess a child's ability to develop a model, a teacher must observe the model development. Checklists or rubrics that include categories both for the modeling process *and* the accuracy of the location and shape of bodies of water would be necessary to accurately assess this particular performance expectation. Teachers can use the constructed-response item strategies and suggestions described previously to help craft effective performance and portfolio assessments. See table 11.1 for an example of a rubric that could be used to assess second graders' models.

Table 11.1

Sample Rubric: 2-ESS2-2		
Criteria	Score (0–3) *Teachers assign a score based on whether the child's work met the given criteria.*	Comments *Teachers provide open-ended comments to explain the score earned.*
Land and water bodies are labeled correctly.		
Shape of land and water bodies is accurate.		
Relative size of land and water bodies is accurate.		

USING RUBRICS AND CHECKLISTS

Rubrics or other scoring guides, such as checklists, are helpful tools to clarify exactly what you're assessing and what students are expected to do. However, not all rubrics are the same and different rubrics can be used for different purposes.

Gonzales (2014b) offers a detailed overview of the different types of rubrics teachers might choose and uses the example of making breakfast in bed as the task being assessed. *Holistic rubrics* are fairly general and include broad characteristics to define each scoring level. These rubrics are used on common standardized assessments such as the writing portion of the SAT exam and allow teachers to read a student's response and quickly assign an overall score. However, they are not specific and don't provide detailed feedback for students. On the other hand, *analytic rubrics* provide detailed descriptions of what a score is for each category. Gonzales (2014b) explains that this type of rubric "breaks down the characteristics of an assignment into parts, allowing the scorer to itemize and define exactly what aspects are strong, and which ones need improvement." Analytic rubrics allow students to see exactly where they met expectations, excelled, or fell short. However, these can be challenging for teachers to create and don't necessarily account for the variety of ways a student might respond to a certain prompt.

Another option for grading open-ended assessments is the single-point rubric. In an earlier piece, "Your Rubric Is a Hot Mess and Here's How to

Fix It," Gonzales (2014c) provides some suggestions for simplifying the grading process. The single-point rubric clearly identifies all the characteristics of a proficient student response (e.g., a "3" on a 4-point scale) so it can be used by students to ensure they've completed each necessary part of the assignment. Teachers then provide feedback on the specific shortcomings or strengths in each category. This single-point rubric is more direct than a holistic rubric in that it lays out all criteria for success but does not require listing each way in which a student could excel or fall short. However, it is more reliant on teacher feedback to be its most successful.

Finally, teachers could also opt for checklists as opposed to rubrics. Checklists are preferred when a project has many parts or requirements that must be completed. For example, if a student were designing an experiment, the checklist would ensure that she included a control group and multiple trials, recorded visual observations, listed numerical measurements, and so on. Checklists can be especially helpful for encouraging students to self-assess their own projects or used in conjunction with a UDL approach for learning as a scaffold. The checklist can aid a child in seeing what has been completed and what still needs to be done.

FORMATIVE ASSESSMENT

Unlike summative assessment, which is typically used to determine a grade, value, or worth, *formative assessment* is also known as assessment *for* instructional decision making. Formative assessment can be an ongoing process invisible to students during which teachers *monitor and adjust* instructional moves. It can take place before or during instruction on a given topic and can include both formal and informal monitoring. If a teacher were to give a test as a summative assessment, then decide to reteach a topic students seemed to struggle with, she is using the summative assessment formatively. Given the detailed format of the NGSS performance expectations and the fact that for many performance expectations ongoing investigations and multiple lessons are necessary to ensure students master the content, teachers must engage in formative assessment before planning any sort of summative measurement of students' learning. Additionally, teachers using an inquiry-based approach steer away from tasks that require rote memorization. In order to guide students throughout their inquiry process, they must receive frequent guidance and feedback from the teacher.

Formative Assessment before Instruction

Before starting a new unit or topic, a teacher might want to get a sense of what students already know about a topic. For example a teacher might use a card sort activity during which she asks students to classify different

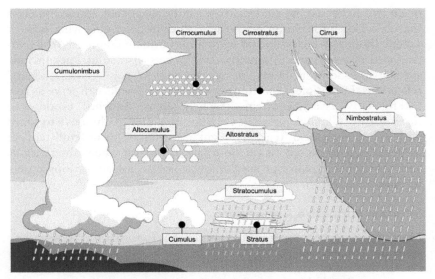

Figure 11.2 Diagram of types of clouds. (Valentin de Bruyn)

photographs of clouds. If it is clear that the students group clouds by shape and type (e.g., cumulus, stratus, and nimbus), the teacher might simply want to review cloud types quickly before moving on to cloud formation or the water cycle. On the other hand, if the students use some other categories (e.g., sunny day clouds and rainy day clouds), the teacher might want to ask some more questions about students' reasoning before beginning the new unit. Formative assessment before instruction can also give the teacher a snapshot of the variety of different levels of understanding students have, which can help in creating groups within the class or identifying which students might need some more assistance or additional learning materials.

Formative Assessment during Instruction

During instruction, teachers should frequently check in to see what their students know. These check-ins can let the teacher know which misconceptions students are holding on to and which ones they've moved past. It can also clarify areas for review, reteaching, or additional time and resources. Teachers can also regroup students and identify which students might need additional classroom support and which ones have already mastered content and might need a challenge.

Formal Formative Assessment

Formal formative assessment is planned formative assessment. It can take many forms such as a written pre-test about an upcoming topic or an exit ticket asking students to describe what they learned in class that day. This information helps the teacher to determine what is most salient about a given lesson and what information might need to be reintroduced or explained differently. Exit tickets also sometimes include specific questions, prompts, or suggestions to help guide students' reflections. Oftentimes, questions in student textbooks can serve as formal formative assessment items. Teachers can use students' responses to these already planned questions to gauge how they might move forward with a class discussion. Teachers might also want to purposefully collect students' science notebooks or journals to monitor their observations and questions or plan out specific questions to ask at various points throughout a lesson.

Informal Formative Assessment

More often, teachers use informal approaches to formatively assess their students. For example, a teacher might ask her students to hold up a certain number of fingers to demonstrate their comfort at certain points in a lesson (i.e., hold up one finger if you're confused, three if you feel like you're starting to understand, and five if you've got it). Similarly the teacher could ask the students to use a thumbs up/thumbs down sign. When students are involved with ongoing investigations, experiments, or projects, teachers can employ a red light/green light approach. Students can keep an index card with a red circle on one side and green circle on the other. When students are feeling comfortable, they can keep the green side facing up, but when struggling or in need of teacher help, they can flip the red side up. This gives the teacher an opportunity to visually scan the classroom to get a sense of where he is most needed.

Exemplar Formative Assessment Strategies

Though we've referenced some simple strategies teachers might use in class, such as exit tickets or using a thumbs up/thumbs down approach, there are many tools teachers can use to assess their students formatively. Page Keeley has written several books on formative assessment tools specific to science. What follows are some examples from her 2008 book, *Science Formative Assessment: 75 Practical Strategies for Linking Assessment, Instruction, and Learning.*

Commit and Toss: Students anonymously respond to a question on a sheet of paper. They crumple the paper into a ball and toss it in front of the room. Each student then retrieves someone else's paper and reads it aloud. This gives the teacher a sense of the variety of ideas held by students in their class.

Muddiest Point: The teacher summarizes what the class has covered in previous lessons. She then asks students to write down which of these ideas is the "muddiest" for them and gets a better idea of which ideas might need reteaching.

Two Stars and a Wish: This strategy is great for exit tickets or for providing feedback on peers' presentations. Students identify two strengths (stars) and one suggestion for improvement (wish).

Annotated Student Drawings: Students can draw or diagram what they know about a particular topic and annotate their drawings to clarify the ways in which ideas are connected to one another or not.

Keeley's (2008) book, along with her other work, provides a detailed description of specific learning goals related to each sample probe and can help teachers to decide which strategies they wish to use in their own teaching.

A CHALLENGE

Let's return to the sentiment in the quotation that started this chapter: without regular check-ins, assessment at the end of instruction only confirms the success of our high-flying students. Imagine it is close to the end of the school year, and you're teaching a kindergarten class about weather and focusing in on the following NGSS performance expectation:

K-ESS2-1. Use and share observations of local weather conditions to describe patterns over time.

As part of your morning activities, your class records data on the local weather in a class weather journal. You have information on precipitation, wind, and temperature for the entire school year so far and the ability to access local weather maps. During the last two weeks of the school year, you plan to cover and then assess this performance expectation.

First, consider what a *measurable behavioral learning objective* might be for this standard.

Next, consider how you might assess that standard summatively. Would you use a written test? Would you want the students to create a diagram? What about a group presentation for the year's weather? What is your reasoning for that decision?

Then, consider what the written assessment or rubric might look like for your summative assessment.

Next, consider what tools you would use for *informal formative assessment* and *formal formative assessment* throughout the two-week science unit.

Finally, anticipate the variety of responses your kindergarteners might have throughout the unit. What plans might you make for reteaching a missed concept?

CONCLUSION

Though sometimes challenging, assessment is a critical piece of teaching across all content areas, and science is no exception. Understanding the historical and theoretical context of assessment in science can help us to situate how it influences our day-to-day interactions in the classroom. Regardless of format, assessment must be purposeful and structured in a way that it measures what students know or have learned. Frequent and ongoing formative assessment is critical for teachers to know what their students have learned and how to adjust instruction to best meet their needs.

12
Science Outside of School

■ ■ ■

Youth frequently engage in powerful science and engineering activities that take place after or outside-of-school. They learn STEM content, engage in STEM practices, and develop an understanding of how STEM is used in the world. To capitalize on those assets, educators and other stakeholders should learn about, leverage, and broker connections for youth across the STEM learning experiences available in and out of school.

—Philip Bell and Bronwyn Bevan, *What is the Role of Informal Science Education in Supporting the Vision for K–12 Science Education?*

When I teach my elementary science methods course, my students participate in a field placement in a local elementary school as part of the class requirements. Though the school, grade, and cooperating teacher can change frequently, I'm certain of one thing about every class my students will visit: in each classroom, there will be at least one dinosaur kid. I challenge my students early on to seek out the dinosaur kid by the end of the semester. Most are successful.

In this chapter, we will discuss principles of learning outside of school settings and why it is important to recognize science learning outside of school. We highlight specific examples of outside-of-school learning environments—everyday learning experiences, designed environments, and programs—along with strategies for integrating students' interests and ideas into the classroom and creating classroom museums.

Figure 12.1 Children visiting dinosaur skeletons at the Museum of Natural History in New York City. (Lauren Madden)

This textbook is dedicated to science teaching and learning in K–6 classroom settings. However, we know that nearly all science learning, especially among young children, takes place outside of school. Whether through Discovery Channel programming or trips to designed environments such as museums and aquaria, much of what children learn about science comes from outside-of-school experiences. Research shows that up to 95 percent of Americans learn science outside of school (Falk & Dierking, 2010). This importance of outside-of-school experiences emphasizes the necessity for teachers to build strong connections to other learning spaces and modalities. Interestingly, Falk and Dierking note that internationally, young children in the US perform similarly to those from other countries on international science tests, while secondary school students fall behind their international counterparts. However, on measures of scientific literacy among adults, those in the US tend to outperform individuals from countries often celebrated as high-achieving in standardized tests such as Korea and Germany. This is especially surprising as only about 30 percent of adults report having taken a college science course. Most adults learn about science through informal or nonformal experiences ranging from hobbies to television programs.

Though most can agree that formal learning is what we think of when we consider traditional school settings, learning that happens outside of school can take a variety of formats sometimes described as nonformal or informal learning. Ainsworth and Eaton (2010) describe *nonformal* learning as experiences that may or may not be intentional but are organized in some way, while *informal* learning experiences rely on experiential learning and spontaneity. For the purpose of this text, we will use the term *informal* to encompass learning in both the informal and nonformal categories.

INFORMAL SCIENCE AND THE NGSS

The National Association for Research in Science Teaching (NARST) provided a statement to guide us in thinking about connections between informal science institutions (ISIs) and the NGSS (Falk et al., 2014). It offers the following three suggestions:

1. ISIs and schools should collaboratively develop goals for supporting NGSS that mutually respect the unique contributions each sector makes to children's science learning.
2. If ISIs are to be assessed within the context of NGSS, such assessments should be designed in ways that are sensitive to the actual focus, scale, and realities of ISI experiences.
3. ISIs should continue to attend to important aspects of public science education such as interest development and lifelong science engagement; outcomes included within the NRC framework but missing from the NGSS.

Finding some clear shared goals and overlaps between formal and informal settings can help create a coherent approach to science learning that considers a broad scope on scientific meaning-making. In a National Research Council report titled *Surrounded by Science: Learning Science in Informal Environments*, Fenichel and Schweingruber (2010) provide more guidance on what informal science learning can be through a structured presentation of the landscape of informal science learning.

Venues for Learning Science outside the Classroom

Everyday learning activities include the hobbies, discussion, entertainment, and sometimes even chores that people engage with in a scientific way (Fenichel & Schweingruber, 2010). This is by far the broadest venue and can include children's observations of worms and leaves when playing in the mud as well as purposeful choices of what kinds of books to read or TV programs to tune into. The majority of individuals' informal science learning experiences can fall into this category, and through careful questioning, teachers can learn more about their students' emerging scientific understandings created as a result of this learning. Everyday learning experiences can also be adapted for the classroom such as through following scientists on Twitter (as discussed in chapters 10 and 11) as a class or individuals or allowing students choice in content delivery (would students prefer to listen to a podcast, read a magazine article, or watch a video about a given science topic?). It can seem distracting at times to respond to each child's comments and contributions about their own scientific interests, but providing mechanisms for children to use their everyday learning experiences helps them better understand the scientific world at large and science content at school. Some schools use concepts like "genius hour" or "preferred activity time" in which time is dedicated to pursue individual interests in the day or week. Exploring science and scientists through everyday experiences can be an excellent use of that choice-based learning time.

In contrast to everyday learning, *designed environments* are places intentionally created to educate in an informal way (Fenichel & Schweingruber, 2010). Museums, parks, zoos, and aquaria are common examples of designed environments where science learning takes place. Visits to these places are often sporadic and tied to a specific context (e.g., going to the zoo on a teacher workday with your parents), unlike everyday learning, which can be more ongoing and connected to hobbies and interests. However, there are many tools in place to extend students' experiences with informal learning environments such as websites and even video cameras of exhibits that can allow visitors to connect with these places over a longer time frame. Teachers can use these tools to help extend the impact of field trip experiences or share their own professional learning with their students. Children across New Jersey and Pennsylvania who visit Duke Farms on a class trip can tune into the Duke Farms Eagle cam[1] before or after their visit to continue their learning on this topic and maintain a relationship with this organization.

A third venue for learning science outside the classroom is *programs* (Fenichel & Schweingruber, 2010). After-school clubs and activities, summer camps, and some citizen science experiences focused on specific topics are programs. Though content deepening is often a goal, they also

---

1. https://www.dukefarms.org/eaglecam.

allow students to connect more closely with scientific enterprise and develop positive attitudes about science. For example, through many science camps, students are able to use tools and techniques to collect and interpret data over time.

Regardless of venue, informal science learning experiences all tend to engage individuals in multiple ways to encourage learning (Fenichel & Schweingruber, 2010). They provide learners with direct experiences with the scientific world, build on visitors' knowledge and interests, and allow for choice in learning.

EVERYDAY LEARNING: JOEY

Joey is an eleven-year-old student in fifth grade and is absolutely the sort of child who comes to mind when we think about children who love science. When asked about his interests in life, Joey's immediate response was: animals and space! His face lit up when he began to explain the books, television programs, and websites he enjoys, which included the Kratts and *National Geographic*. Joey loves to talk about animals. He loves thinking and telling others about both the rules and patterns in nature, such as the way animals use scents or pheromones to communicate, *and* the exceptions to those rules that make certain animals unique, such as the way eels find and catch their prey. He can offer detailed descriptions of big cats' teeth and lemurs' movement with an easy smile. He has a wealth of knowledge and interest and is always eager to share what he's learned. Sometimes, Joey is able to share this knowledge in traditional school settings but not often in a way that allows him to build connections between his everyday knowledge and the school-based science instruction. In chapter 4 of this text, we discussed scientific habits of mind and the nature of science. Joey's everyday learning about patterns and exceptions in nature can serve as a rich foundation for understanding what science is and isn't. With this sort of foundation, he is well prepared to build connections to more complex ideas both inside and outside of school. Teachers have a great opportunity to use purposeful student-centered approaches to leverage the extensive knowledge that Joey and children like him possess as a scaffold in their teaching but must be willing to ask good questions and modify their plans.

When asked about his future goals, Joey explained that he hopes to work with all kinds of animals in the wild—and to become an astronaut. With the right supports, his curiosities and dispositions set him up well for success as a scientist.

Figure 12.2 Joey observing an exhibit at an aquarium. (Tabitha
Dell'Angelo)

DESIGNED ENVIRONMENTS: THE FRANKLIN INSTITUTE

Located in central Philadelphia, the Franklin Institute is a world-famous science museum that has been in operation since 1824. This museum's visitors range from the general public and tourists visiting the city to children exploring with their school classes or summer camp groups. The group sales department works closely with teachers and school administrators to ensure that the group visit is tailored to fit the needs of the teachers both logistically and in terms of content the children visiting will be exposed to. The museum itself hosts a multitude of exhibits—some are permanent, such as the famous two-story model of a human heart that visitors can walk through. Other exhibits, such as one about Pixar animations, rotate through science museums around the world. Throughout the Franklin Institute, one can also interact with rotating live science demonstrations, view IMAX films, and visit a planetarium. In order to ensure the visitors' experience is worthwhile and meaningful, a rotating schedule of volunteers and full-time employees circulate to lead demonstrations and provide explanations for guests. Yet the reach of the Franklin Institute is much larger than just the exhibits and events within the building itself. Through hosting summer camps to coordinating programs that connect local middle and high schoolers to internships in labs at universities throughout the greater Philadelphia area, the museum seeks to

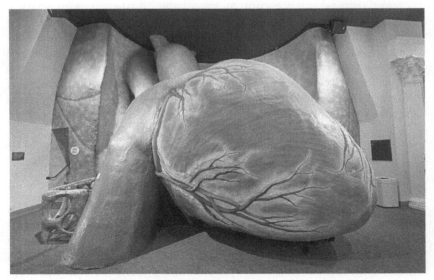

Figure 12.3 Human heart model at the Franklin Institute in Philadelphia. (Superx308)

spark curiosity about science far and wide. In addition, the museum hosts events such as *Science After Dark* where adults can visit and learn from scientists in a casual and relaxed setting. Even during times of crisis, such as the 2020 COVID-19 outbreak, opportunities for visitors to virtually visit exhibits or learn from partner scientists at the Franklin Institute abounded. The Institute's chief bioscientist, Dr. Jaytri Das, hosts regular webinars and posts information about the disease itself, as well as other interesting and engaging scientific topics.

Teachers can use their own visits to the Franklin Institute for professional development as well. The visits alone provide meaningful opportunities to engage in science. They can also demonstrate strategies to present information in intriguing ways, and teachers can glean advice on content presentation from their own experiences. The Franklin Institute hosts a number of research-based professional development efforts in which teachers and schools can join ongoing events organized by the institute's professional development team. Much of this work, led by Julia Skolnik, focuses on educating teachers about neuroscience and connects directly to the Franklin Institute's brain exhibit. This focus on neuroscience allows teachers to uncover ideas about how students think as well as about the science of the brain itself.

It should be clear that although they hope to teach visitors about science, the goal of all the work at the Franklin Institute is *not* to increase visitors' science content knowledge. Rather, it is to spark a sense of wonder and encourage interest and curiosity. Much of their work is grounded on the idea of building visitors' *science capital*, or the thoughts, knowledge, ideas, and connections an individual has related to science (Archer et al., 2015). By providing engaging scientific experiences for individuals, the Franklin Institute increases the chances of those individuals making scientifically informed decisions and perhaps further exploring scientific interests or careers.

PROGRAMS: PARKWAY ELEMENTARY SCHOOL'S ENVIRONMENTAL STEM CLUB

Teachers Jill Voorhees, Debra Cornelius, Howard Taylor, Sara Tink, and Nicole Siegel meet with a group of sixty-seven students grades K–5 from Parkway Elementary School in Ewing, New Jersey, in their courtyard garden. Club members are grouped by grade (K–1, 2–3, and 4) and meet regularly with teachers to explore their school's courtyard. Fifth graders serve as leaders and assist their teachers throughout the club meetings. Each week these students take on a new task from planting and weeding to maintain their school's garden to building new structures or installing art. This year, they've paid close attention to sustainability and the use

Figure 12.4 Teachers and students working in Parkway Elementary School's courtyard garden in the environmental STEM club. (Jill Voorhees)

of the engineering design process when building. Throughout the club meetings, students use science process skills like observation, prediction, and measurement. They regularly investigate ongoing questions about where to locate certain plants or which animals regularly visit the garden. The club members have many opportunities to compare and contrast, wonder, and use creativity. This program allows children to *do* science without the constraints of a classroom and as a result sparks interest in the world around them and develops a deeper connection to their sense of place. Teachers take on the role of "guide on the side" facilitating students' conversations, encouraging them to think deeply, and allowing students to see them as multifaceted individuals.

Fenichel and Schweingruber (2010) offer a framework called *Strands of Informal Science Learning* that helps informal educators think purposefully

Strands of Informal Science Learning
STRAND 1 – Sparking Interest and Excitement Experiencing excitement, interest, and motivation to learn about phenomena in the natural and physical world.
STRAND 2 – Understanding Scientific Content and Knowledge Generating, understanding, remembering, and using concepts, explanations, arguments, models, and facts related to science.
STRAND 3 – Engaging in Scientifc Reasoning Manipulating, testing, exploring, predicting, questioning, observing, and making sense of the natural and physical world.
STRAND 4 – Reflecting on Science Reflecting on science as a way of knowing, including the processes, concepts, and institutions of science. It also involves reflection on the learner's own process of understanding natural phenomena and the scientific explanations for them.
STRAND 5 – Using the Tools and Language of Science Participation in scientific activities and learning practices with others, using scientific language and tools.
STRAND 6 – Identifying with the Scientific Enterprise Coming to think of oneself as a science learner and developing an identity as someone who knows about, uses, and sometimes contributes to science.

Figure 12.5 Strands of Informal Science Learning based on Fenichel and Schweingruber (2010)

about the design and implementation of their work. Though not every learning experience addresses each strand, these are a useful organizing structure for thinking about informal science learning holistically.

Challenge: consider the cases above describing examples of everyday learning, designed environments, and programs. How were students involved in each of those examples engaging with the strands of informal science learning?

THE OPPORTUNITY GAP: WHY INFORMAL SCIENCE LEARNING DESERVES ATTENTION

As discussed earlier, research shows that more than 95 percent of science learning occurs outside of school settings (Falk & Dierking, 2010). As a result, children who lack opportunities to engage in informal science learning often have a decrease in science achievement as measured by standardized tests or even sometimes class grades. Lum (2016) reports on national studies that indicate that the science achievement gap is often apparent between White and Black students as early as kindergarten, before any formal school-based learning has taken place. Yet, Falk and Dierking note, decision-makers often try to address this gap through working to improve school science. In some cases, such as those discussed by Li, Klahr, and Siler (2006), the resulting in-school science instruction toward test preparation focused on simply recalling definitions rather than engaging with authentic science learning. Though well-funded, those efforts are often counterproductive, as the amount of time allotted for and dedicated to science learning is small, especially at the elementary level, where national studies indicate that as little as twenty minutes per day are dedicated to the subject (Trygstad, 2013). This type of science instruction focused on test preparation and memorization fails to support students in developing science capital and exacerbates the opportunity gap.

Perhaps one way of addressing the "achievement" gap is to focus on providing *opportunities* for authentic science engagement inside and outside the classroom. Lum (2016) discusses the opportunity gap that we see as early as kindergarten as one in which everyday science experiences are quite different among groups. Parent surveys that accompanied this study indicated some clear differences in the way parents could influence science learning too: "Within families, parents who regularly talk and interact with toddlers can point out and explain physical, natural, and social events occurring around them daily. This might help youngsters learn facts and concepts that will prepare them to take better advantage of science instruction they receive during elementary and middle school."

Yes, encouraging parents to engage in scientific talk with children can be helpful for mediating this gap—but it is only one part of the solution. (See chapter 10 of this text for some strategies for engaging families with science learning.) However, we must also acknowledge the knowledge honed from everyday science learning that many children have. We cannot assume that there *must* be some sort of deficit in children who perform poorly on tests. Perhaps the tests aren't written in a way that accesses their understanding. As we discussed in chapter 2 of this text, *all* children are naturally curious. Yet not all children have the language or internal tool kits for expressing what they know and understand about the natural world, especially in the early years. Many prominent educational researchers (e.g., Delpit, Ladson-Billings) have discussed the difference between home language and school or formal language. Gonzales

(2014a) offers some advice on helping students to learn how to *code switch*, or "change one's language, dialect or speaking style to better fit one's environment." Gonzales does not suggest that teachers should reject children's nonstandard English use. Rather, she offers some practical strategies for helping children see and hear more formal/standard ways of expressing information. A simple example would be that a child might describe the fog in the bathroom after a hot shower or bath as a cloud in the bathroom. The teacher could recognize what the student noticed— "Yes, it does look like a cloud"—and then introduce a more scientifically acceptable term—"In science we call that cloudy-looking stuff steam or water in the gas phase." This is especially critical for science teaching and learning where everyday terms have different meanings in scientific settings (see chapter 10 for an example using the term *compare*).

Imagine a young kindergartener observed a "roly poly" or pillbug on the playground rolling into a ball. She might have spent the entire recess period watching the way the insect interacted with its environment, engaging in careful observation. Rather than writing this experience off as typically childish, a teacher could acknowledge the child's science skills during recess. She could name the terms *observation*, *organism*, and *environment*. She could help the student use descriptive language about size, shape, texture, and interaction with her finger. Doing so could help the child draw on her own prior experiences outside of school and express an interest in naming them in a scientific way. In addressing the kindergartener in this way, we are helping to build her science capital as well as increasing her chances to interact with the world in a scientifically literate way.

So what can we, as formal educators in K–6 settings, do to help reduce this opportunity gap?

- First and foremost, teachers must become curious about students' scientific interests! Asking children, especially young children, about what they like to do and helping them to identify the ways in which they are scientific is a great start. Providing them with the science language we use to describe these kinds of interactions is a great next step. Honoring what students know and are already bringing with them to the classroom is essential; giving it a name simply makes it easier to measure their knowledge and for them to connect with others using the language of science.
- Another strategy is to work with after-school programs to engage students in science learning outside the classroom. Much like the team at Parkway Elementary School was able to structure informal learning through their environmental STEM club, teachers

can work alongside school leaders to ensure this sort of programming exists at their own schools.

- Teachers can and should develop relationships with informal learning environments through visiting on their own, planning school trips, and engaging in professional learning. Modeling the process of learning yourself can help students to take risks in their own learning and inspire them to expand their own boundaries. These types of relationships can also help teachers to create ongoing informal learning for their students through interacting virtually with museum websites or live animal cameras in the classroom. On a more local level, building relationships with local libraries or parks can help expand children's science learning "worlds" beyond the scope of their classroom.

- Teachers can create informal learning environments within their own classroom. Lee (2019) offers suggestions for having a student-led museum in the classroom to allow children to identify and tell the story of interesting objects. These experiences help children to hone storytelling skills and better describe their interactions with the world around them.

- Finally, where possible, integrate student interests into your standard science instruction. One benefit of the NGSS is that they are broad and adaptable. If you are studying force and motion, it is just as easy to use toy cars as it is to use carts, but student engagement will change considerably when the lesson materials are based on student interests.

CONCLUSION

If nothing else, find the dinosaur kid. Make sure you, as the teacher and trusted adult, know your students. Be willing to help guide their journeys to better understand the parts of the world they find interesting, and help them name them and use the skills they build to connect to a broader and more formal audience.

13

Advocating for Science

■ ■ ■

Teachers are trusted adults who spend a great deal of time with hundreds or even thousands of children throughout the course of their careers. They are responsible for helping students sort out the differences between fact and fiction and helping students research questions and determine whether a resource is reliable. In science, this can be a great task.

In this chapter, we wrap up the book by emphasizing ways to advocate for science and advocate using science. We look at the way science is portrayed in the media, then identify strategies for unpacking these media messages. Finally, we summarize how other parts of this text can provide teachers with support in science advocacy.

Media is ubiquitous, and almost everywhere we look we can see signs of scientific information being misrepresented. Take, for example, the headlines that came up for me when I recently searched on Google for "science says chocolate is healthy," pages with titles such as "7 Proven Benefits of Dark Chocolate" and "Science Says Eating Chocolate Every Day Is Good for You."

Though of course I wish it were true, we can't simply agree that information is accurate because a headline says so. With just a little closer look at one of these articles, titled "Dark Chocolate Is Now a Health Food. Here's How That Happened," we can see that the findings aren't quite what we might guess from the title. This article details an ongoing attempt by chocolate makers around the world to fund positive scientific studies about chocolate. These studies have taken place around the world, attempting to capitalize on health benefits of cocoa supported by unbiased science. But, as Belluz (2017) noted, "Despite the industry effort to date, cocoa still has never been proven to carry any long-term health benefits. And when it's delivered with a big dose of fat and sugar, any potential health perks are very quickly outweighed by chocolate's potential harm to the waistline."

This is just one example of sensational science headlines designed to sell products and entice readers. Comedian John Oliver covered the topic several years ago on a segment of his HBO program *Last Week Tonight*.[1] In this funny but informative video, Oliver pokes fun at the way scientific information is manipulated by the media and shares some broader-scale implications for this phenomenon. For example, people might ignore the preponderance of evidence we have about vaccine efficacy, climate change, and evolution if they were presented only with partial information, sensationalized reporting, or biased studies, such as those done by industries with a financial stake in the research.

Yet information can be misleading and sometimes altered to appear accurate to the casual reader. Some commonly used tactics are downplaying sample size (e.g., calling something a "trend" that occurs in just a few individuals), extrapolating beyond the data (e.g., assuming that findings in a study using mice apply directly to humans), or creating a title that is similar to a reputable source (e.g., *Science American* sounds a lot like the respected journal *Scientific American*). Farrar (2017) suggests using a four-step process (GLAD) to help determine the accuracy of scientific studies reported in the media. These steps are:

1. Get past the clickbait.
2. Look out for crazy claims.
3. Analyze sources.
4. Determine outside expert opinions.

This process is simple to use and can help teachers clarify their own understandings and help their students do the same. For children conducting research in a classroom or informal learning setting, this framework can be helpful in selecting credible resources to cite.

On the flip side, teachers can also guide their students in using science as a tool for decision-making and understanding. Take the example of starting a school garden. Students can use science to guide decisions

---

1. https://www.vox.com/2016/5/9/11638808/john-oliver-science-studies-last-week -tonight. Note: language in this story is not appropriate for classroom use.

about a multitude of questions that will come up during the planning and implementation process such as:

- Where to plant the garden? Students can look at soil saturation, hours of light vs. shade, soil type, and proximity to the school building to help make a decision.
- What to plant? Students can research which plants are native to the area and best suited for the soil and light in the garden. Students can also research whether flowers or vegetables would be a better choice by sending out surveys to classmates and community members.
- How to cook the vegetables? Students can couple Internet research about the types of cooking that maximize the nutrient content with surveys of their peers to select recipes and cooking methods.

In order to use science to "fact check" news stories or make a case for a place-based learning initiative, teachers must feel confident in their own abilities to facilitate these experiences. As a result, teachers need access to reputable resources. As we mentioned in chapter 9, NSTA's website offers a wealth of information such as guidelines for teaching controversial topics or the *Science and Children* Science 101 section that provides adult-level content on a variety of topics. We also mentioned reaching out to scientists through social media such as Twitter or TikTok. If confusing things arise, don't hesitate to ask an expert for some clear information to guide your next steps. Scientists who have opted to make their work public through social media are typically eager to interact with children and teachers and contribute to their learning! And children should see you go through this process. It is critical that children learn that the adults in their lives are not all-knowing but rather information-seeking beings just like them.

ADVOCATING FOR A CAUSE

Aside from scientific advocacy for its own sake to help students develop skills in argumentation and determine the validity of resources, students should be empowered to use science to advocate for themselves and their interests. This does not have to be a controversial process—advocating for a school garden using science is an example of evaluating information and using that process to make decisions. Students should also be given opportunities to use science to advocate for things that matter to them.

Connecting across Content Areas

Thinking back to chapters 7 and 8 in this text—how can we connect science to other content areas? At various points in every grade, children write essays, letters, and reports for the purpose of persuading others. This is an excellent opportunity to use science and literacy together in a meaningful way. For example, the Advocate for Animals organization allows students to research endangered or threatened species and write letters requesting elected officials or other citizens to protect them.[2]

Elementary schools oftentimes have less than healthy choices available in the cafeteria, and lunches often include food that many children discard. A walk past many school cafeteria trash bins can reveal mealy apples, rubbery cheese sticks, and bags of pre-cut carrots. Students can use science to advocate for changing school lunch menus and use math to help. By simply weighing food waste and recording data, students can use this information to make a case for changing menus. Further, students could also use math to sort waste into trash, compost, and recycling.

Current Events and Relevant Issues

Children might also express interest in current events such as the massive wildfires across the continent of Australia or the hurricanes affecting the Caribbean. Students can use their scientific argumentation skills alongside art, literacy, mathematics, and social studies to create posters to spread awareness for these issues, set up fundraisers, or pair up with a "sister" class in one of the affected locations. Using science content to make sense of these events is especially powerful in reducing fear and misinformation around ideas that might seem complex and abstract.

Having a student with a terminal illness is a teacher's worst nightmare. However, many teachers find themselves in this situation. Using science to better understand the illness can help calm classmates and foster empathy. For example, many students think of cancer as a disease that killed a family member. If, on the other hand, a teacher described the process of cells dividing uncontrollably, students might be more willing to think critically about how systems affect one another within the human body and develop empathy for a suffering classmate through better understanding.

STEPS FOR CLASSROOM PRACTICE

Using science and science teaching as a tool for advocacy can seem like a daunting process, but reviewing some key points from each chapter of this text can make it a possibility.

1. Recognize the strengths children bring to your classroom. Students are never empty vessels and come with a wealth of prior knowledge waiting to be activated.

---

2. https://www.doinggoodtogether.org/advocate-for-animal.

2. Allow children to explore and make sense of their ideas before providing a "correct" answer. Short-circuiting their learning processes can take the wonder out of science.
3. Make sure students are clear on what is and isn't science. There are qualities, characteristics, and processes that define the discipline and make it a unique way of knowing and understanding the world.
4. Ensure that your use of the NGSS standards is comprehensive. Content should not be taught in isolation of process. Children need a chance to connect knowledge across domains and engage in the act of doing science while learning.
5. Think carefully and purposefully when planning lessons and activities. It is critical to have a clear learning goal in mind before writing a lesson and to ensure that you are able to collect data to use as evidence as to whether students were able to meet the goal you set out.
6. Connect science to other disciplines, especially ELA and mathematics. The skills that span across disciplines such as prediction and inference are habits of mind that are critical for developing scientific literacy.
7. Solve problems using science and sometimes engineering. Realistic and authentic problem-solving allows children to apply their knowledge outside specific classroom contexts and think holistically about the world around them.
8. Use science to unpack socioscientific issues and argumentation to support claims with evidence and reasoning.
9. Create an equitable learning environment that honors the contributions of all students. Support learners with inclusive examples and class materials that are adaptable.
10. Assess both formatively and summatively regularly, ensuring that your assessments match the broader learning goals and not simply what is easy to test.
11. Build connections between formal and informal science for all children. These connections are the foundation of scientific understanding.

Science is a process, product, and enterprise. It is a discipline that grows and corrects itself over time. It allows students to explore big questions about how the world works. It is your job to make sure that science is a verb and something that students are actively doing.

Glossary

∎ ∎ ∎

504 plan A plan developed to ensure that a child who has a disability identified under the law and is attending an elementary or secondary educational institution receives accommodations that will ensure their academic success and access to the learning environment.

accommodation Altering one's existing schemas, or ideas, as a result of new information or new experiences. This concept is associated with the work of educational theorist Jean Piaget.

achievement tests Used after students have completed learning a given topic to provide information on what they may have learned.

action and expression (UDL) Giving students multiple models for how they can show what they know and providing support, examples, and feedback frequently.

analytic rubrics Provide specific guidance for each category of a given assessment.

aptitude tests Used to predict future performance. Placement tests and diagnostic tests fall into this category.

argumentation Systematic process of evaluating a claim.

assessment Any systematic procedure for collecting information that can be used to make inferences about the characteristics of people or objects.

assets-based perspective One focused on strength; views diversity in thought, culture, and traits as positive traits.

assimilation The cognitive process of making new information fit in with your existing understanding. This concept is associated with the work of educational theorist Jean Piaget.

Bloom's Taxonomy   System for classifying questions with respect to cognitive challenge. The revised version of this taxonomy has new labels for each level but serves the same purpose of classifying difficulty in questions.

citizen science   Scientific endeavors in which the general public engage in collecting and/or analyzing data as part of a larger research effort.

claim   A statement based on systemic observation and evidence.

code switch   To change one's language, dialect, or speaking style to better fit one's environment.

confirmatory investigation   Investigations that follow prescribed steps and procedures.

constructivism   The idea that children construct knowledge through observation and interaction with the world around them. This concept is associated with the work of educational theorist Jean Piaget.

criterion-referenced test   Test that compares test-takers' scores to a set of predetermined criteria.

data   Information collected using specific methods for a specific purpose of studying or analyzing.

decoding   Understanding the relationship between a symbol and an idea.

deficit perspective   Attributes many children's school failures to perceived deficits within the children, their families, and their cultures.

designed environments   Places intentionally created to educate in an informal way such as zoos or museums.

enclothed cognition   The influence of clothing on the way individuals think, feel, and function, in areas like attention, confidence, or abstract thinking.

engagement (UDL)   Providing options for students to engage, acknowledging that not every child's interest will be sparked by the same phenomenon.

engineering design process   Process used by engineers to develop solutions.

epistemology   A theory of knowledge or way of understanding the world.

everyday learning   Learning activities that include the hobbies, discussions, entertainment, and sometimes even chores that people engage with in a scientific way.

evidence   Data used in the service of a claim (i.e., to support or refute a claim).

fact   Observation that has been repeatedly confirmed and for all practical purposes is accepted.

formative assessment   Assessment for instructional decision-making.

growth mindset   Belief that one's talents and abilities can expand with hard work and practice.

guided inquiry   Investigations in which the teacher selects the topic and develops the questions, but the students design procedures.

high-stakes test   Test in which the outcomes have direct consequences for schools, teachers, or students, such as ranking, funding, or parental choice in student placement.

holistic rubrics   General guides that can be applied to multiple topics and provide broad categories and characteristics for assessment.

inclusion   The concept of placing children who require special education services alongside their more typical peers for all or most of the school day.

individualized education plan (IEP)   A plan or program developed to ensure that a student who has a disability identified under the law and is attending an elementary or secondary educational institution receives specialized instruction and related services.

informal learning   Experiences relying on experiential learning and spontaneity.

learning objectives   Specific measurable and behavioral descriptions of what students will learn or do in a lesson.

maximum performance tests   Measure the upper limits of a test-taker's ability or knowledge such as speed tests or power tests.

nonformal learning   Experiences that may or may not be intentional but are organized.

norm-referenced test   Test that compares test-takers' scores to a set of norms.

norms   Patterns of outcomes on a test.

open inquiry   Investigations in which the students develop the questions and procedure, while the teacher selects the overall topic.

opinion   A view or judgment formed about something, not necessarily based on fact or knowledge.

opportunity gap   The fact that arbitrary factors such as where someone was born (zip code), race, ethnicity, and socioeconomic status determine many of his or her opportunities for success inside and outside the classroom.

place-based learning   An immersive learning experience that leverages culture, heritage, ecosystems, and/or geological features in a given place.

productive questions   Questions that stimulate critical thinking about science in children.

productive struggle   Allowing students to work through a challenge independently or in small groups before offering scaffolding or support.

programs   Informal learning experiences such as clubs or meetings centered on science learning outside of school.

progressive education   Instruction that engages children in hands-on learning experiences and builds upon children's prior knowledge. This concept is associated with the work of educational theorist John Dewey.

qualifiers   Stipulations based on time or other factors associated with the claim.

reasoning   Using data as evidence to support or refute claims.

representation (UDL)   Using multiple media and supports to present content.

scaffolding   The process by which teachers structure an activity to allow children to work within their zone of proximal development. This concept is associated with the work of educational theorist Lev Vygotsky.

schema   Units of knowledge or mind maps. This concept is associated with the work of educational theorist Jean Piaget.

science capital   The thoughts, knowledge, ideas, and connections an individual has related to science.

science concepts   Terms used to describe abstractions and fundamental ideas that help to understand phenomena. Examples include "force," "evaporation," "moon phases," and "cell division."

social constructivism   The idea that knowledge is constructed through social interaction. This concept is associated with the work of educational theorist Lev Vygotsky.

standardization sample   Subset of test-takers used as a point of comparison for scores and to determine norms.

standardized tests   Are administered, scored, and interpreted in a standardized manner in order to make comparisons among large groups of students.

structured inquiry   Investigations in which the teacher selects the topic and develops the procedures and questions.

test   The device or procedure used to obtain information about an individual, and often that information has to do with her behavior, knowledge, or ability in a given context.

theory   A well-supported and agreed-upon framework or explanation for an aspect of the natural or designed world.

zone of proximal development (ZPD)   The gap between what an individual can do on his or her own and what he or she can do with the assistance of a more capable other. This concept is associated with the work of educational theorist Lev Vygotsky.

References

■ ■ ■

Abdi, S. W. (2006). Correcting student misconceptions. *Science Scope, 39.*

Ainsworth, H. L., & Eaton, S. E. (2010). *Formal, non-formal and informal learning in the sciences.* Calgary: Onate Press.

American Association for the Advancement of Science (AAAS). (2013). *Project 2061.* Retrieved November 11, 2019 from: http://www.project2061.org/pub lications/sfaa/.

Archer, L., Dawson, E., DeWitt, J., Seakins, A., & Wong, B. (2015). "Science capital": A conceptual, methodological, and empirical argument for extending Bourdieusian notions of capital beyond the arts. *Journal of Research in Science Teaching, 52*(7), 922–48.

Atkin, J. M., & Karplus, R. (1962). Discovery or invention? *The Science Teacher, 29*(5), 45–51.

Banchi, H., & Bell, R. (2008). The many levels of inquiry. *Science and Children, 46*(2), 26.

Bell, M. (2017). For this Vatican astronomer, the solar eclipse is divine coincidence. WUNC. Retrieved October 31, 2019, from: https://www.wunc.org/post /vatican-astronomer-solar-eclipse-divine-coincidence.

Bell, P. & Bang, M. (2015). *Overview: How can we promote equity in science education?* STEM Teaching Tools #15. Retrieved from: http://stemteaching tools.org/assets/landscapes/STEM-Teaching-Tool-15-Equity-Overview.pdf.

Bell, P., & Brevan, B. (2015). *What is the role of informal science education in supporting the vision for K–12 science education?* STEM Teaching Tools #38. Retrieved from: http://stemteachingtools.org/assets/landscapes/STEM-Teach ing-Tool-38-Role-of-Informal-Ed.pdf.

Belluz, J. (2017). Dark chocolate is now a health food. Here's how that happened. *Vox.* Retrieved from: https://www.vox.com/science-and-health/2017/10 /18/15995478/chocolate-health-benefits-heart-disease.

Bernard, S. (2010). Neuroplasticity: Learning physically changes the brain. *Eduto-pia*. Retrieved from: https://www.edutopia.org/neuroscience-brain-based-learn ing-neuroplasticity.

Bossé, M. J., Lee, T. D., Swinson, M., & Faulconer, J. (2010). The NCTM process standards and the five Es of science: Connecting math and science. *School Science and Mathematics*, 110(5), 262–76.

Bronfin, D. R. (2008). Childhood immunization controversies: What are parents asking? *The Ochsner Journal*, 8(3), 151.

Brown, S. (2004). Integrating math and science. *Classroom Leadership*, 7(6). Retrieved from: http://www.ascd.org/publications/classroom-leadership/mar 2004/Integrating-Math-and-Science.aspx.

Brunsell, E. (2010). The five features of science inquiry: How do you know. *Edutopia*. Retrieved from: https://www.edutopia.org/blog/teaching-science-inquiry -based.

Bulgren, J., & Ellis, J. (2015). The argumentation and evaluation guide: Encouraging NGSS-based critical thinking. *Science Scope*, 38(7), 78.

Bybee, R. W. (2014). The BSCS 5E instructional model: Personal reflections and contemporary implications. *Science and Children*, 51(8), 10–13.

Carrier, S. J., Jones, M. G., Ennes, M., Madden, L., Lee, T., Cayton, E., Chesnutt, K., Huff, P., Phillips, L., & Bellino, M. (2020). Stereotypes of scientists: Seeds of progress and recommendations for elementary teachers. *Science Educator*, 27(2), 1–7.

Cartlidge, E. (2015). Talking science and God with the pope's new astronomer. *Science*. Retrieved from: https://www.sciencemag.org/news/2015/09/talking -science-and-god-popes-new-chief-astronomer.

CAST (2018). *Universal design for learning guidelines version 2.2*. Retrieved from: http://udlguidelines.cast.org.

Covey, S. R. (2013). *The 7 habits of highly effective people: Powerful lessons in personal change*. New York: Simon and Schuster.

Davis, D., & Tiller Smith, T. (2020). Incorporating anti-racism in elementary science. NSTA. Retrieved from: https://www.nsta.org/blog/incorporating-anti -racism-elementary-science.

DeBoer, G. (2019). *A history of ideas in science education*. New York: Teachers College Press.

Dell'Angelo, T. (2017). *Butterflies: The strange and real story of how a caterpillar turns into a butterfly*. Self-published.

Dewey, J. (1916). *Democracy and education*. New York: Macmillan.

———. (1929). *The question for certainty*. New York: Minton.

Duran, L. B., & Duran, E. (2004). The 5E Instructional Model: A learning cycle approach for inquiry-based science teaching. *Science Education Review*, 3(2), 49–58.

Dweck, C. (2015). Carol Dweck revisits the growth mindset. *Education Week*, 35(5), 20–24.

Edupress. (2017). *Quick Flip questions for the revised Bloom's Taxonomy*. Garden Grove, CA: Teacher Created Resources.

Eisenkraft, A. (2003). Expanding the 5E model. *The Science Teacher*, 70(6), 56–59.

Elstgeest, J. (2001). The right question at the right time. In W. Harlen (Ed.), *Primary science: Taking the plunge. How to teach science more effectively for ages 5 to 12.* Portsmouth, NH: Heinemann.

Erickson, K. (2019). *NASA Science Space Place.* Retrieved October 31, 2019, from: https://spaceplace.nasa.gov/science/en/.

Falk, J., & Dierking, L. D. (2010). The 95 percent solution: School is not where most Americans learn most of their science. *American Scientist, 98*(6), 486.

Falk, J., & Drayton, B. (2004). State testing and inquiry-based science: Are they complementary or competing reforms? *Journal of Educational Change, 5*(4), 345–87.

Falk, J., Osborne, J., & Dorph, R. (2014). Supporting the implementation of the Next Generation Science Standards (NGSS) through research: Informal science education. NARST. Retrieved from: https://narst.org/blog/ngss-informal-education.

Farrar, L. (2017). Can you spot bad science reporting? KQED. Retrieved from: https://ww2.kqed.org/education/2017/03/01/can-you-spot-bad-science-reporting/.

Fenichel, M. F., & Schweingruber, H. A. (2010). *Surrounded by science: Learning science in informal environments.* Washington, DC: National Academies Press.

Finson, K. D., Ormsbee, C. K., & Jensen, M. M. (2011). *Differentiating science instruction and assessment for learners with special needs, K–8.* Thousand Oaks, CA: Corwin Press.

Geier, R., Blumenfeld, P. C., Marx, R. W., Krajcik, J. S., Fishman, B., Soloway, E., & Clay-Chambers, J. (2008). Standardized test outcomes for students engaged in inquiry-based science curricula in the context of urban reform. *Journal of Research in Science Teaching, 45*(8), 922–39.

Ghose, T. (2013). "Just a theory": 7 misused science words. *Scientific American.* Retrieved from: https://www.scientificamerican.com/article/just-a-theory-7-misused-science-words.

Godsey, M. (2018). How podcasts can improve literacy in the classroom. *Common Sense.* Retrieved from: https://www.commonsense.org/education/articles/how-podcasts-can-improve-literacy-in-the-classroom.

Golden, B., Grooms, J., Sampson, V., & Oliveri, R. (2012). Generating arguments about climate change. *Science Scope, 35*(7), 26.

Gonzales, J. (2014a). Know your terms: Code switching. *Cult of Pedagogy.* Retrieved from: https://www.cultofpedagogy.com/code-switching/.

———. (2014b). Know your terms: Holistic, analytic, and single-point rubrics. *Cult of Pedagogy.* Retrieved from: https://www.cultofpedagogy.com/holistic-analytic-single-point-rubrics/.

———. (2014c). Your rubric is a hot mess; here's how to fix it. *Brilliant or Insane.* Retrieved from: http://www.brilliant-insane.com/2014/10/single-point-rubric.html.

Hardiman, M. M., JohnBull, R. M., Carran, D. T., & Shelton, A. (2019). The effects of arts-integrated instruction on memory for science content. *Trends in Neuroscience and Education, 14,* 25–32.

Hood River Middle School. (2015). Place-based learning: A multifaceted approach. *Edutopia*. Retrieved from: https://www.edutopia.org/practice/place-based-learning-connecting-kids-their-community.

Horowitz, R. (2004). *Crab moon*. Somerville, MA: Candlewick Press.

Iared, V. G., Oliveira, H. T. D., & Reid, A. (2017). Aesthetic experiences in the Cerrado (Brazilian savanna): Contributions to environmental education practice and research. *Environmental Education Research, 23*(9), 1273–90.

Ippolito, J., Condie, C., Blanchette, J., & Cervoni, C. (2018). Learning science and literacy together. *Science and Children, 56*(4), 91–95.

Johnson, B. (2011). How to creatively integrate science and math. *Edutopia*. Retrieved from: https://www.edutopia.org/blog/integrating-math-science-creatively-ben-johnson.

Johnson, C., & Hanegan, N. (2006). No Child Left Behind. *Science Scope: Teachers Toolkit*. Retrieved from: https://www.nsta.org/publications/news/story.aspx?id=52797.

Kahn, S. (2019). *It's still debatable! Using socioscientific issues to develop scientific literacy K–5*. Arlington, VA: NSTA.

Karplus, R., & Butts, D. P. (1977). Science teaching and the development of reasoning. *Journal of Research in Science Teaching, 14*(2), 169–75.

Karsnitz, J., O'Brien, S., & Hutchinson, J. (2012). *Engineering design: An introduction*. Clifton Park, NY: Cengage Learning.

Keeley, P. (2008). *Science formative assessment: 75 practical strategies for linking assessment, instruction, and learning*. Thousand Oaks, CA: Corwin.

Konicek-Moran, R., & Keeley, P. (2015). *Teaching for conceptual understanding in science*. Arlington, VA: NSTA.

Lederman, N. (2014). Nature of science and its fundamental importance to the vision of the Next Generation Science Standards. *Science and Children, 52*(1), 8–10. doi:10.2505/4/sc14_052_01_8.

Lee, E. J., & Hanuscin, D. (2014). Taking the "mystery" out of argumentation. *Science and Children, 52*(1), 46.

Lee, L. (2019). Creating a student-run museum in your classroom. *Edutopia*. Retrieved from: https://www.edutopia.org/article/creating-student-run-museum-your-classroom.

Li, J., Klahr, D., & Siler, S. (2006). What lies beneath the science achievement gap: The challenges of aligning science instruction with standards and tests. *Science Educator, 15*(1), 1–12.

Liem, T. L. (1987). *Invitations to science inquiry*. Chino Hills, CA: Science Inquiry Enterprises.

Lindahl, A. (2019). Science language for all. *Rethinking Schools, 34*(2). Retrieved from: https://www.rethinkingschools.org/articles/science-language-for-all.

Long, S. (2019). Diversity is what makes it interesting to study living things. *Rethinking Schools, (34)*1. Retrieved from: https://www.rethinkingschools.org/articles/diversity-is-what-makes-it-interesting-to-study-living-things.

Love, B. (2021). How to make anti-racism more than a performance. *Education Week*. Retrieved from: https://www.edweek.org/leadership/opinion-empty-promises-of-equity/2021/01.

Lum, L. (2016). The consequences of poor science education in kindergarten. *The Atlantic*. Retrieved from: https://www.theatlantic.com/education/archive/2016/02/how-poor-science-knowledge-in-kindergarten-spells/471312/.

Madden, L., Blatt, C., Ammentorp, L., Kneis, D., & Stanton, N. (in press). From science in the art gallery to art in the science classroom: Using arts-integrated professional development to enhance environmental education. *Journal of College Science Teaching*.

Madden, L., & Joshi, A. (2013). What does culture have to do with teaching science? *Science and Children*, 51(1), 66.

Madden, L., Peel, A., & Watson, H. (2014). The poetry of dandelions: Merging content-area literacy and science content knowledge in a fourth-grade science classroom. *Science Activities*, 51(4), 129–35.

Madden, L., & Turner, J. (2018). Enhancing gifted early elementary students' learning experiences through engineering design: One teacher's experience. In K. Taber, M. Sumida, & L. McClure (Eds.), *Teaching gifted learners in STEM subjects: Developing talent in science, technology, engineering, and mathematics*. London: Routledge.

Madden, L., & Wiebe, E. N. (2013). Curriculum as experienced by students: How teacher identity shapes science notebook use. *Research in Science Education*, 43(6), 2567–92.

Malzahn, K. A. (September 2013). *2012 national survey of science and mathematics education—status of elementary school mathematics teaching*. Retrieved on October 9, 2013, from: http://www.horizon-research.com/reports/?sort=report_category.

McTighe, J., & Wiggins, G. (2012). *Understanding by design framework*. Alexandria, VA: Association for Supervision and Curriculum Development.

Mensah, F. M. (2015). Multiculturalism. In R. Gunstone (Ed.), *Encyclopedia of science education*. Dordrecht, Netherlands: Springer.

Muir, R. (2019). TikToks are teaching Generation Z about science. *Massive Science*. Retrieved from: https://massivesci.com/notes/science-communication-tiktok-social-media-education-outreach-squid-genes/.

NASA. (January 9, 2020). *Do scientists agree on climate change?* Retrieved from: https://climate.nasa.gov/faq/17/do-scientists-agree-on-climate-change/.

National Art Education Association. (April 2014). Position statement on STEAM education. Retrieved from: https://www.arteducators.org/advocacy/articles/552-naea-position-statement-on-steam-education.

National Research Council (NRC). (1996). *National Science Education Standards*. Washington, DC: National Academies Press. https://doi.org/10.17226/4962.

———. (2007). *Taking science to school: Learning and teaching science in grades K–8*. Washington, DC: National Academies Press.

———. (2012). *A framework for K–12 science education: practices, crosscutting concepts, and core ideas*. Washington, DC: National Academies Press. https://doi.org/10.17226/13165.

———. (2013a). Appendix D: All standards, all students. *The Next Generation Science Standards*. Washington, DC: National Academies Press. https://www

.nextgenscience.org/sites/default/files/resource/files/Appendix%20G%20-%20 Crosscutting%20Concepts%20FINAL%20edited%204.10.13.pdf.

———. (2013b). Appendix F: Science and engineering practices. *The Next Generation Science Standards*. Washington, DC: National Academies Press. https://www.nextgenscience.org/sites/default/files/resource/files/Appendix %20G%20-%20Crosscutting%20Concepts%20FINAL%20edited%204 .10.13.pdf.

———. (2013c). Appendix G: Crosscutting concepts. *The Next Generation Science Standards*. Washington, DC: National Academies Press. https://www .nextgenscience.org/sites/default/files/resource/files/Appendix%20G%20-%20 Crosscutting%20Concepts%20FINAL%20edited%204.10.13.pdf.

———. (2013d). *Monitoring progress toward successful K–12 STEM education: A nation advancing?* Washington, DC: National Academies Press.

———. (2013e). *The Next Generation Science Standards*. Washington, DC: National Academies Press. http://www.nextgenscience.org/.

National Science Foundation, National Center for Science and Engineering Statistics. (2015). *Women, minorities, and persons with disabilities in science and engineering: 2015. Special Report NSF 15-311*. Arlington, VA: NSF. Available at http://www.nsf.gov/statistics/wmpd/.

National Science Teaching Association (NSTA). (2013). Position statement on the teaching of evolution. Retrieved from: https://www.nsta.org/about/positions /evolution.aspx.

———. (2014). About the Next Generation Science Standards. Retrieved November 14, 2019, from: https://ngss.nsta.org/About.aspx.

———. (2018a). Position statement on the teaching of climate science. Retrieved from: https://www.nsta.org/about/positions/climatescience.aspx.

———. (2018b). Transitioning from scientific inquiry to three-dimensional teaching and learning. Retrieved from: https://www.nsta.org/about/positions/3d.aspx.

NYU Steinhart School of Culture, Education, and Human Development. (2018). An asset-based approach to education: What it is and why it matters. Retrieved from: https://teachereducation.steinhardt.nyu.edu/an-asset-based-approach-to -education-what-it-is-and-why-it-matters/.

Petroff, A. (2017). The exact age when girls lose interest in science and math. *CNN Tech*. Retrieved from: https://money.cnn.com/2017/02/28/technology /girls-math-science-engineering/index.html.

Piaget, J. (1964). Cognitive development in children. *Journal of Research in Science Teaching*, 2(2), 176–86.

Reynolds, C., Livingston, R., and Wilson, V. (2009). *Measurement and assessment in education, second edition*. Hoboken, NJ: Pearson.

Rose, D. L. (2019). *Scientists get dressed*. Apex, NC: Persnickety Press.

Rosen, J. (2018). Black students who have one black teacher are more likely to go to college. Johns Hopkins Hub. Retrieved from: https://hub.jhu.edu/2018 /11/12/black-students-black-teachers-college-gap/.

Sanders, M. (December/January 2009). STEM, STEM education, STEM mania. *The Technology Teacher*, 20–26.

Thurs, D. (2015). That the scientific method accurately represents what scientists do. In R. L. Numbers & K. Kampourakis (Eds.), *Newton's apple and other myths about science*. Cambridge, MA: Harvard University Press.

Trygstad, P. J. (September 2013). *2012 national survey of science and mathematics education—status of elementary school science teaching*. Retrieved on October 9, 2013, from: http://www.horizon-research.com/reports/?sort=report_category.

Understanding Evolution (n.d.). Nature of science. Retrieved November 4, 2019, from: https://evolution.berkeley.edu/nature/index.shtml.

Vogler, K. E. (2008). Asking good questions. *Educational Leadership, 65*(9).

Volk, D., & Long, S. (2005). Challenging myths of the deficit perspective: Honoring children's literacy resources. *Young Children, 60*(6), 12–19.

Vygotsky, L. (1987). *Thinking and speech*. In R. W. Rieber & A. S. Carton (Eds.), *The collected works of Vygotsky, volume 1: Problems of general psychology*. New York: Plenum. (Original work published 1934).

Warshauer, H. K. (2015). Strategies to support productive struggle. *Mathematics Teaching in the Middle School, 20*(7), 390–93.

Wells, G. (September 1994). Learning and teaching "scientific concepts": Vygotsky's ideas revisited. Vygotsky and the Human Sciences Conference, Moscow.

Wenner, J. A., & Galaviz, S. (2020). Science packs. *Science and Children, 57*(5), 35–39.

Wiggins, G. P., & McTighe, J. (2005). *Understanding by design*. Alexandria, VA: Association for Supervision and Curriculum Development.

Withers, S., Brown, H., and Tate, W. K. (1920). The dandelion. In *The child's world: Primer, volume 3*. Richmond, VA: BF Johnson Publishing Co.

WNYC Studios. (June 2014). The goo and you. *Radiolab* [audio podcast]. Retrieved from: https://www.wnycstudios.org/podcasts/radiolab/segments/goo-and-you.

Wong, D., Pugh, K., & the Dewey Ideas Group at Michigan State University. (2001). Learning science: A Deweyan perspective. *Journal of Research in Science Teaching, 38*(3), 317–36.

You, H. S. (2017). Why teach science with an interdisciplinary approach: History, trends, and conceptual frameworks. *Journal of Education and Learning, 6*(4), 66–77.

Index

■ ■ ■

AAAS. *See* American Association for the Advancement of Science

Abdi, S. W., 68

accommodation, 20, *20*

acetone experiment, 41

achievement tests, 148

action: and expression in UDL, 144, 145; questions, 64–65

activity: Commit and Toss, 156–57; cookie, 4–6, *5*; ice cube, *28*, 28–29, 87; mixture separation, 24–25, *25*

Adequate Yearly Progress (AYP), 149

Advocate for Animals, 176

advocating, for science, 3–4, 119–32, 173–77

AES. *See* Argumentation Evaluation Strategy

after-school programs, 162–63, 165–66, 170–71

American Association for the Advancement of Science (AAAS), 54

analysis, of apples, 18

analytic rubrics, 153

anti-racist teaching, 139–40

apple analysis, 18

apprenticeship, 24

aptitude tests, 148

architecture, UDL in, *143*

argumentation, scientific, 121–22

"The Argumentation and Evaluation Guide" (Bulgren and Ellis), 121

Argumentation Evaluation Strategy (AES), 121

"Arkansas Mom Obliterates Common Core" (video), 52

art: communication and, 110, *110*; community building and, 111, *111*; content explanation and, 111–12

ask (engineering design process), 98

assessment, 148–49, 152–58, 177; summative, 147; teacher-created, 150–51

assets-based perspective, 141–42

assimilation, 20, *20*

Atkin, J.M., 34

attention-focusing questions, 64

AYP. *See* Adequate Yearly Progress

backward design: stage 1 of, 69, *70*, 71; stage 2 of, *70*, 71; stage 3 of, *70*, 72

Banchi, H., 30–31
Bang, M., 134
basic questions, of science, 40–41
Battleship, 87–88
beaver dam project, 100, *101*
Bell, Philip, 134, 159
Bell, R., 30–31
Belluz, J., 174
Benchmarks for Science Literacy
(AAAS), 42, 54
benzene, 3
Best (Mrs.), 31
Bevan, Bronwyn, 159
Biodiversity Discovery and Phenology
project, 136, 138
Bloomberg, Alyssa, 129
Bloom's Taxonomy, 65, *65*; revision
of, 66
Bossé, M. J., 86
Boston Museum of Science, 108
Bronfin, D. R., 125
Brown, S., 86
Brunsell, E., 33
"The BSCS 5E Instructional Model"
(Bybee), 34, 35
building, on previous knowledge of
children, 170, 176
Bulgren, J., 121
Bush, George W., 149
Butterflies (Dell'Angelo), 85
Bybee, Richard, 34, 35

cake analogy, for NGSS, 55, *55*–56
"Can You Spot Bad Science
Reporting?" (Farrar), 174
CAST. *See* Center for Applied Special
Technology
cause-and-effect relationships, 57
CCSS-M. *See* Common Core State
Standards in Mathematics
Center for Applied Special Technology
(CAST), 142
challenge: circuit, 22; controversial
topics, 126; discrepant events,
36; flowers or vegetables, 122;
individual assets, 142; mealworm,

19; NGSS, 62, 67, 145; paper
tower, 24; scientific engagement,
6; STEM, 107; weather, 157–58
Chan, Benny, 127, *128*
change. of outdated terms, 138
checklists, 154
child development, 16–22
"Childhood Immunization
Controversies" (Bronfin), 125
children: doing science as, 1–2; drones
and, 15–16; prior knowledge
of, 22; scientific interaction of,
1–2, 22, 24; scientific interests
of, 170–71; understanding of
phenomena of, 19; waiting room
toys and, 6
Children's Hospital of Philadelphia,
125–26
chocolate, 173–74
choice-based learning time, 162
citizen science, 131–32, 136–37
citizenscience.gov, 136
claim, in scientific argumentation, 121
clarification statement, 60
classification, description and, 6
climate change, 123–25
clouds, 155, *155*
cognitive: dissonance, 36; skills, 17
Cold War, 32, 53
collection, of shells, 1, *2*
Commit and Toss activity, 156–57
Common Core State Standards
(CCSS), 59, *59*
Common Core State Standards in
Mathematics (CCSS-M), 52–53
common practices in the NGSS, CCSS
and, 59, *59*, 81, *81*, *84*
communication, arts integration and,
110, *110*
community building, art and, 111,
111
"compare," scientific use of, 140–41,
150, 170
comparison questions, 64
compost project, 108, *109*
concepts, science, 33

confirmatory investigations, 30, 33
connection, of science to language
    arts, mathematics and, 79–88,
    89, 177
Consalmango, Guy, 40, 126
"The Consequences of Poor Science
    Education in Kindergarten"
    (Lum), 169
constructed-response items, 151; tools
    for, 152
constructivism, 20
content: explanation arts and, 111–
    12; knowledge test taking skills
    contrasted with, 151; storylines,
    62
continental drift, 43
The Continuum of Inquiry, 30, 30–31
controversial topics, in science,
    123–25
cookie activity, 4–6, 5
Cookie Chemistry, 5, 6, 7, 7–9, 25;
    Handout I for, 10, 10–11, 11;
    Handout II for, 12, 12–13, 13
Cornelius (Mrs.), 122
Cornell Ornithology lab, 131
"Correcting Student Misconceptions"
    (Abdi), 68
Covey, Stephen, 69–70
COVID-19, 166
Crab Moon (Horowitz), 83
create (engineering design process),
    98
"Creating a Student-Run Museum in
    Your Classroom" (Lee), 171
creative expression, science and, 112,
    112
credit, for scientific discoveries, 47
criterion-referenced tests, 148–49
crosscutting concepts, 57–58
culture: school as testing-centric, 104;
    science and, 47, 59, 81; science
    integrated with, 139, 141
current events, 176
curricula, standards contrasted with,
    53, 62
Curry, Judith, 123–24

dandelion exercise, 83, 84
dangers, of inquiry-based teaching,
    36–37
"Dark Chocolate Is Now a Health
    Food. Here's How That
    Happened" (Belluz), 173–74
Das, Jaytri, 166
Davis, D., 139–40
DCIs. See Disciplinary Core Ideas
DeBoer, George, 32
decoding, of texts, 85
deficit perspective, 141
DeLeo, Ava, 129
Dell'Angelo, Tabitha, 85
Democracy and Education (Dewey),
    19
description, classification and, 6
design: backward, 69; process
    engineering, 98
designed environments, 162, 165–66,
    171
development, of child, 16–22
developmentally appropriate science,
    16–17
Dewey, John, 16, 18–19, 32
diagrams, usefulness of, 37
diatoms, 113, 114, 114–17
Dierking, L. D., 160, 169
Differentiating Science Instruction
    and Assessment for Learners with
    Special Needs, K–8 (Finson), 142
dinosaur kid, 159, 160, 171
Disciplinary Core Ideas (DCIs), 4–5,
    55–57, 105, 105–6, 106; climate
    change as, 124
Discovery Channel, 160
"Discovery or invention?" (Atkin and
    Karplus), 34
discrepant events, 36, 41
diversity, in science education, 133,
    134–41
"Diversity Is What Makes it
    Interesting to Study Living
    Things" (Long), 141
doing science, as children, 1–2
domain-specific explanations, 17, 17n1

drones, children and, 15–16
Dylan, Bob, 104

Earth and Human Activity, *106*
education: progressive, 18; standards
    in, 51, *52*
The Educational Forum (journal), 123
Edupress flip book, 66
efficacy, of vaccines, 125–26
ELA. *See* English Language Arts
electric circuits, 22
Elementary and Secondary Education
    Act (ESEA), 149
ELL. *See* English Language Learners
Ellis, J., 121
Elstgeest, J., 64
empirical evidence, 43
enclothed cognition, 131
encouragement, of exploration, 17
Encyclopedia of Science Teaching, 139
Engage (5E Learning Cycle), 34, 46
engagement, with science, 6, 17, 19,
    29, 63; opportunities for, 169–71;
    representation and, 136; in UDL,
    144, 145
Engineering, Technology, and
    Application of Science (ETS),
    105, 105–6, *106*
Engineering Design (Karsnitz), 98
engineering design process: 5E
    Learning Cycle Contrasted with,
    107; steps of, 98, *99*, 100
Engineering is Elementary (Boston
    Museum of Science), 108
English Language Arts (ELA), 59
English Language Learners (ELL),
    141
environmental STEM club, 166–67,
    167
environments, designed, 162
epistemology, 39, 40, 44–45
equity, equality *versus*, *133*
equity, in science education, *133*,
    134–41, 145
ESEA. *See* Elementary and Secondary
    Education Act

ETS. *See* Engineering, Technology, and
    Application of Science
Evaluate (5E Learning Cycle), 35
events, discrepant, 36, 41
everyday learning activities, 161–62,
    163
evidence, in scientific argument, 121–22
evolution, 125–26
exercise, dandelion, 83, *84*
experience of subject, for meaningful
    learning, 18–19
experiment: acetone, 41; graduated
    cylinder, 22; hippy milk, *48*,
    48–49; insulation, 68; mealworm,
    19, *19*; owl pellet, 45; paper
    tower, 24; plant, 107; pollen, 56;
    sunlight, 82; surface of Earth, 31
Explain (5E Learning Model), 35
explanations, domain-specific, 17,
    17n1
exploration, encouragement of, 17
Explore (5E Learning Cycle), 34–35
Extend (5E Learning Cycle), 35
extending and lifting model, 67

failure, STEM and, 104
Falk, J., 160, 169
family engagement, 138, 169
Farrar, L., 174
Fenichel, M. F., 161, 167–68, *168*
Finson, K. D., 142
5E Learning Cycle, 27, 35, *35*, 72,
    86; engineering design process
    contrasted with, 107
504 plans, 150
"The Five Features of Science Inquiry"
    (Brunsell), 33
flowers or vegetables challenge, 122
formal formative assessment, 155–56,
    157
format, of NGSS, 60–61, *61*
formative assessment, 147; formal,
    155–56, 157; informal, 156,
    157; before instruction, 154–55;
    during instruction, 155; strategies
    for, 156–57

formulation of questions, for science teaching, 63–64
foundations, of inquiry-based science, 32
A Framework for K-12 Science Education (NRC), 54–55, 58
Franklin, Rosalind, 40
The Franklin Institute, *165*, 165–66

Galaviz, S., 138
gaps, opportunity, 134
"Generating Arguments about Climate Change" (Golden), 124
geologic time, 37
Ghose, T., 44
GLAD method, for determining accurate sources, 174
Godsey, M., 85
Golden, B., 124
Golden Ratio, 45–46, *46*
Gomez (Mr.), 68
Gonzales, Jennifer, 153–54, 169–70
"The Goo and You" (podcast), 85
graduated cylinder experiment, 22
groups, structure of, 24
growth mindset, 104
guided inquiry, 31

Hagan, Marguerita, 113
Halley's Comet, 47, 54
heart model, *165*
high-stakes test, 149, 150
hippy milk experiment, *48*, 48–49
history, of inquiry in United States, 27, 32
A History of Ideas in Science Education (DeBoer), 32
holistic rubrics, 153
home language, school language contrasted with, 169–70
Hood River Middle School, 131
Horowitz, R., 83
"How Podcasts Can Improve Literacy in the Classroom" (Godsey), 85
"How to Creatively Integrate Science and Math" (Johnson), 86

"How to Make Anti-Racism More than a Performance" (Love), 139
human endeavor, science as, 47

ice cube activity, *28*, 28–29, 87
IDEA. *See* Individuals with Disabilities Education Act
IEP. *See* individualized education plan
imagine (engineering design process), 98
improve (engineering design process), 98
inclusion, in science education, *133*, 134–41, 142–45
inclusive instruction, 141, 142, 146, 177
"Incorporating Anti-Racism in Elementary Science" (Davis and Tiller Smith), 139–40
individualized education plan (IEP), 149
Individuals with Disabilities Education Act (IDEA), 149–50
informal: formative assessment, 156, 157; learning, 161, 171, 177
informal science institutions (ISIs), 161
inquiry, scientific, 29
inquiry-based teaching, 27–34; dangers of, 36–37
inquiry model, phases of, 35–36
instruction, inclusive, 141
insulation experiment, 68
"Integrating Math and Science" (Brown), 86
integration, of art into science, 108–12, *109*, *110*, *111*, *112*
integration, of science and culture, 139, 141
interdisciplinary instruction, 79
investigations, confirmatory, 30
Ippolito, J., 83–84
ISIs. *See* informal science institutions
items: constructed response, 151–52; selected-response, 150–51
It's Still Debatable! (Kahn), 122–23

Joey (student), 163, *164*
Johnson, B., 86
Jones (Mr.), 22
"Just a Theory" (Ghose), 44

Kahn, S., 122–23
Karplus, R., 34
Karsnitz, J., 98
Keeley, Page, 33, 156–57
knitted yoga mat, *112*, 113
knowledge, of science, 3, 43
"Know Your Terms: Code Switching."
    (Gonzales), 153, 170
"Know Your Terms: Holistic, Analytic,
    and Single-Point Rubrics"
    (Gonzales), 153
Konicek-Moran, R., 33

lake diatom project, 113
Lamoreaux, Karen, 52
language, Vygostsky and, 23
language arts and mathematics,
    connection of science to, 79–80
language arts instruction, nonfiction
    texts in, 83
Last Week Tonight (TV program), 174
leaf cleanup project, 100, *102, 103*
learning objectives, 68–69, 157
"Learning Science" (Wong), 18
"Learning Science and Literacy
    Together" (Ippolito), 83–84
Lederman, N., 45
Lee, L., 171
lesson plans, 71–72, 177
limitations, of scientists, 47
literacy, scientific, 3
Long, S., 141
Love, Bettina, 139
Lum, L., 169

Madden, Lauren, 83, 123
Malzahn, K. A., 80
"The Many Levels of Inquiry" (Banchi
    and Bell, R.), 30–31
mathematics, science and, 86
maximum performance tests, 148

McGee, Earyn, 136, *137*
McTighe, J., 69, *70*
mealworm experiment, 19, *19*
measurable behavioral learning
    objective, 157
*Measurement and Assessment in
    Education* (Reynolds), 148
measuring and counting questions, 64
media representation, of scientific
    discoveries, 173–74
Mendel, Gregor, 40
methods, of scientific investigations,
    32, 39, 42; GLAD, 174; Volger,
    66–67
mindset, growth, 104
misconceptions, 67–68
mixture separation activity, 24–25, *25*
models, for learning: BSCS 5E, 34, 35;
    extending and lifting, 67; heart,
    165; inquiry, 35–36
the montillation of traxoline, 29, *29*, 64
Muir, R., 127
multicultural approach, to science
    instruction, 139

NAEA. *See* National Art Education
    Association
NARST. *See* National Association for
    Research in Science Teaching
NASA Space Place, 40
National Art Education Association
    (NAEA), 108
National Association for Research in
    Science Teaching (NARST), 161
National Council for Teachers of
    Mathematics (NCTM), 86
National Education Association
    (NEA), 53, 125
National Research Council, 17, 54,
    57, 59
*National Science Education
    Standards*, 42
National Science Education Standards
    (NSES), 54
National Science Foundation (NSF),
    53, 98, 134, 145

National Science Teachers Association (NSTA), 27–28

National Science Teaching Association, 41, 55, 107, 125, 126; as fact-checking tool, 175

natural systems, order and consistency in, 45

nature of science (NOS), 39, 41, 177

"Nature of Science and its Fundamental Importance to the Vision of the Next Generation Science Standards" (Lederman), 45

NCLB. *See* No Child Left Behind

NCTM. *See* National Council for Teachers of Mathematics

"The NCTM Process Standards and the Five Es of Science" (Bossé), 86

NEA. *See* National Education Association

neuroscience, 79, 166

new evidence, revision and, 43

New York Science Teachers Association database, 68

Next Generation Science Standards (NGSS), 4, 4n1, 6, 25, 42; appendix D of, 133; appendix F of, 59; appendix G of, 57–58; appendix I of, 107; benefits of, 51; cake analogy for, 55, 55–56; challenge, 62, 145, 167; connection to math and language arts standards of, 88–89, *89*; format of, 60–61; history of, 54–55; ISIs and, 161; reading of, 60; STEM and, 105, *105*

NGSS. *See* Next Generation Science Standards

NGSS Performance Expectations, 6, 31, 37, 55, 56; challenge, 62, 67, 145; ETS, *105*, 105–6, *106*; format of, 60–61, *61*; integration of language arts and, 80–82; mathematics and, 87–88; questions and, 67

No Child Left Behind (NCLB), 149

nondogmatic nature, of science, 48, 120, 132

nonfiction texts, in language arts instruction, 82–83

NOS. *See* nature of science

NSES. *See* National Science Education Standards

NSF. *See* National Science Foundation

NSTA. *See* National Science Teachers Association

The Ochsner Journal (journal), 125

Oliver, John, 174

open inquiry, 31

opportunity gaps, 134, 146, 169–71

order and consistency, in natural systems, 45–46

outdated terms, change of, 138

outdoor classroom project, 122

Overview (Bell, P., and Bang), 134

owl pellet experiment, 45

Paddle for the Edge project, 131

Pangea, 43

paper tower experiment, 24

Parkway Elementary School, 166

perspective: assets-based, 141–42; deficit, 141

Pestorius, Morgan, 113

phases of inquiry model, 35–36

Piaget, Jean, 16, 20, 22, 32, 145; time frames of, *21*

pillbug, 170

Pinterest, 28, 29

place-based learning, 129, 131

placement tests, 148

plan (engineering design process), 98

plant experiment, 107

plastic reduction project, 129, *130*

podcasts, in science instruction, 85, 129

The Poetry of Dandelions (Madden), 83

pollen experiment, 56

portfolio or performance assessments, 152

principles, of UDL, 143–44
prior knowledge, of children, 22
problem-posing questions, 65
problem-solving, 177
productive: questions, 64; struggle, 104
progressive education, 18
project: beaver dam, 100, 101; compost, 108, 109; lake diatom, 113; leaf cleanup, 100, 102, 103; outdoor classroom, 122; Paddle for the Edge, 131; plastic reduction, 129, 130; Urban Heat Island Mapping, 136
pseudoscience, 45
Pumpkin Bots, 15

qualifier, in scientific argumentation, 121
quality, of water, 3–4
The Question for Certainty (Dewey), 18
questions: action, 64–65; productive, 64

Radiolab (podcast), 85, 129
reading, of NGSS, 60–61
Rehabilitation Act (1973), 149–50
relationships, cause-and-effect, 57
representation: in science, 134, 135, 136; UDL, 144, 145
research topics, based on interests of students, 129
Revised Bloom's Taxonomy, 66
revision, new evidence and, 43
Reynolds, C., 248
Rose, Deborah Lee, 131
rubrics, 153, 153
Ryan (Mrs.), 108

Sagan, Carl, 39
Sarah (student), 68
scaffolding, 24
schema, 20
school garden, 174–75
school lunch menus, 176

Schweingruber, H. A., 161, 167–68, 168
science: advocation for, 3–4, 119–132, 173–77; basic question of, 40–41; concepts, 33; controversial topics in, 123–25; creative expression and, 112, 112; developmentally appropriate, 16–17; engagement with, 6, 17, 19, 29, 63, 136, 169–71; engineering contrasted with, 107, 113; engineering practices and, 58–60; as explanation of phenomena, 3, 42, 43–44; as human endeavor, 47; instruction podcasts in, 85, 129; integration of art into, 108–12, 109, 110, 111, 112; knowledge of, 3, 43, 47–48; on natural and material world, 47–48; nondogmatic nature of, 48, 120; outside school, 159–69; packs, 138; religion and, 126; representation in, 134, 135; as way of knowing, 44–45
Science, Technology, Engineering, and Mathematics (STEM), 80, 97–98; challenge, 107; in elementary classrooms, 100, 101; failure and, 104; resources for, 107–8
Science, Technology, Engineering, Art, and Mathematics (STEAM), 80, 97–98, 108–13
Science After Dark (event), 166
Science and Children (National Science Teaching Association), 107, 127, 175
Science for All Americans (AAAS), 54, 127
Science Formative Assessment (Keeley), 156–57
"Science Packs" (Wenner and Galaviz), 138
scientific: argumentation, 121–22; concepts systemic features of, 23; discoveries media representation of, 174; engagement challenge, 6; inquiry, 29; interaction of

children, 1–2, 22, 24; interests of
children, 170–71; investigations
variety of methods of, 42;
literacy, 3, 54, 160; method, 32,
39; reasoning, 119–20; theories
laws and, 44, *44*, 119–20; use
of terms and everyday use
differences between, 140–41, 150,
170; vocabulary, 140
"That the Scientific Method
Accurately Represents What
Scientists Do" (Thurs), 39
scientists: in classroom, 127;
limitations of, 47
Scientists Get Dressed (Rose), 131
seal, caught in plastic, *110*
selected-response items, 150; tools for,
151
*Seven Habits of Highly Effective
People* (Covey), 69–70
shells, collection of, 1, *2*
skills, cognitive, 17
Skolnik, Julia, 166
Skype a Scientist (program), 129
Smith (Ms.), 82
Snapshot Safari, 138
social constructivism, 23
socioscientific issues (SSIs), 122–23,
177
"A Song for Our Warming Planet"
(song), 111
Springs Eternal (Madden), 110, 113
SSIs. *See* socioscientific issues
stage 1 (backward design), 69, 70, 71
stage 2 (backward design), 70, 71
stage 3 (backward design), 70, 72
standardized tests, 148, *149*
standards: curricula contrasted with,
53, 62; in education, 51, *52*;
history of, 53
statement, clarification, 60
STEAM. *See* Science, Technology,
Engineering, Art, and
Mathematics
STEM. *See* Science, Technology,
Engineering, and Mathematics

STEM resources, 107–8
Strands of Informal Science Learning
(Fenichel and Schweingruber),
167–68, *168*
strategies, for assessment, 156–57
"Strategies to Support Productive
Struggle" (Warshauer), 104
Strauss, Claude-Levi, 27
structure, of groups, 24
structured inquiry, 31
struggle, productive, 104
student exploration, telling concepts
contrasted with, 30
summative assessment, 147
sunlight experiment, 82
supplementary lesson: Battleship
Wind Farm, *93*, 93–95; Cookie
Chemistry, 7, 7–13, *10*, *11*, *12*,
13; Horseshoe Crabs, *90*, 90–92;
Ride or Diatom, *114*, 114–17;
Termite Trails, *73*, 73–78, *77*, *78*
Surrounded by Science (Fenichel and
Schweingruber), 161
systemic features, of scientific
concepts, 23

Taking Science to School (National
Research Council), 17
teacher-created assessment, 150–51
Teachers Pay Teachers, 28, 29
teaching: anti-racist, 139–40; inquiry-
based, 27
"Teaching for Conceptual
Understanding in Science"
(Konicek-Moran and Keeley), 33
"Teaching Science Is a Sacred Act"
(Madden), 123
technology, in science instruction,
132
telling concepts, student exploration
contrasted with, 30
terminal illnesses, science as tool to
understand, 176
testing, of different materials, 6
testing-centric, school culture as, 104
tests, achievement, 148

test-taking skills, content knowledge contrasted with, 151
texts, decoding of, 85
"The 95 Percent Solution" (Falk and Dierking), 160, 169
theory, scientific concept of, 44, *44*, 119–20
Thinking and Speech (Vygotsky), 22
three-dimensional model, of learning, 55
Thunberg, Greta, 119, *120*, 123
Thurs, D., 39
TikTok, 127, 175
Tiller Smith, T., 139–40
time frames, of Piaget, *21*
tools: for teachers, 127; Vygosky and, 23
Trygstad, P. J., 80
"2012 National Survey of Science and Mathematics, Education" (Malzahn), 80
Twitter, 162, 175

UDL. *See* Universal Design for Learning
understanding, of reason behind scientific processes, 58
Understanding by Design (Wiggins and McTighe), 69–70
Understanding Evolution group, 40–41
understanding of phenomena, of children, 19
United States, history of inquiry in, 27, 32
Universal Design for Learning (UDL), 134, 142, *143*, 146–46, 150; principles of, 143–44, *144*

University of Geneva Archives, 20
Urban Heat Island Mapping Project, 136
US. *See* United States
use, of NGSS, 61–62

vaccine efficacy, 125–26
Vaccine Makers Project, 125–26
Volger (questions method), 66–67
Volk, D., 141
Vygotsky, Lev, 16, 22, 145; tools and language and, 23

Warshauer, H. K., 104
water: distribution paper clips and, 82; quality, 3–4
Water Bar, 111, *111*
weather challenge, 157–58
Wegener, Alfred, 43
Wenner, J. A., 138
What Is the Role of Informal Science Education in Supporting the Vision for K–12 Science Education? (Bell, P., and Bevan), 159
Wiggins, Grant, 69, 70, 147
Women, Minorities, and People with Disabilities in Science and Engineering (NSF), 134, 145
Wong, D., 18
World War II, 53
Wow in the World (podcast), 129

"Your Rubric Is a Hot Mess and Here's How to Fix It" (Gonzales), 153–54

Zone of Proximal Development, *23*, 23–24

About the Author

■ ■ ■

Dr. Lauren Madden is a professor of elementary science education in the Department of Elementary and Early Childhood Education at The College of New Jersey in Ewing, New Jersey. She also coordinates the Environmental Sustainability Education minor and graduate certificate. She holds a BA in earth sciences-oceanography, an MS in marine science, and a PhD in science education. In January 2021, she was recognized as the Association for Science Teacher Education (ASTE) Outstanding Science Teacher Educator of the Year and the NJ STEM Pathways' inaugural I-Can STEM Role Model. Dr. Madden teaches courses in science teaching methods, environmental science, and trends in education. Her teaching and research broadly focus on advocating for scientific literacy and the health of our planet. She has published more than forty peer-reviewed journal articles and book chapters in science and environmental education and regularly presents at research conferences and professional development events across the country. She lives in Lawrenceville, New Jersey, with her husband, Mike; twin sons, Connor and Luke; dog, Macaroni; and cat, Red Sauce.

Milton Keynes UK
Ingram Content Group UK Ltd.
UKHW010701040224
437221UK00010B/69